# CONFRONTING THE IRANIAN CHALLENGE

## HEARING

BEFORE THE

## COMMITTEE ON FOREIGN AFFAIRS
## HOUSE OF REPRESENTATIVES

ONE HUNDRED FIFTEENTH CONGRESS

SECOND SESSION

MAY 8, 2018

### Serial No. 115–126

Printed for the use of the Committee on Foreign Affairs

Available: http://www.foreignaffairs.house.gov/, http://docs.house.gov, or http://www.gpo.gov/fdsys/

U.S. GOVERNMENT PUBLISHING OFFICE

30–016PDF      WASHINGTON : 2018

## COMMITTEE ON FOREIGN AFFAIRS

EDWARD R. ROYCE, California, *Chairman*

CHRISTOPHER H. SMITH, New Jersey
ILEANA ROS-LEHTINEN, Florida
DANA ROHRABACHER, California
STEVE CHABOT, Ohio
JOE WILSON, South Carolina
MICHAEL T. McCAUL, Texas
TED POE, Texas
DARRELL E. ISSA, California
TOM MARINO, Pennsylvania
MO BROOKS, Alabama PAUL
COOK, California SCOTT
PERRY, Pennsylvania RON
DeSANTIS, Florida
MARK MEADOWS, North Carolina
TED S. YOHO, Florida
ADAM KINZINGER, Illinois
LEE M. ZELDIN, New York
DANIEL M. DONOVAN, JR., New York
F. JAMES SENSENBRENNER, JR.,
  Wisconsin
ANN WAGNER, Missouri
BRIAN J. MAST, Florida
FRANCIS ROONEY, Florida
BRIAN K. FITZPATRICK, Pennsylvania
THOMAS A. GARRETT, JR., Virginia
JOHN R. CURTIS, Utah

ELIOT L. ENGEL, New York
BRAD SHERMAN, California
GREGORY W. MEEKS, New York
ALBIO SIRES, New Jersey
GERALD E. CONNOLLY, Virginia
THEODORE E. DEUTCH, Florida
KAREN BASS, California
WILLIAM R. KEATING, Massachusetts
DAVID N. CICILLINE, Rhode Island
AMI BERA, California
LOIS FRANKEL, Florida
TULSI GABBARD, Hawaii
JOAQUIN CASTRO, Texas
ROBIN L. KELLY, Illinois
BRENDAN F. BOYLE, Pennsylvania
DINA TITUS, Nevada
NORMA J. TORRES, California
BRADLEY SCOTT SCHNEIDER, Illinois
THOMAS R. SUOZZI, New York
ADRIANO ESPAILLAT, New York
TED LIEU, California

AMY PORTER, *Chief of Staff*     THOMAS SHEEHY, *Staff Director*
JASON STEINBAUM, *Democratic Staff Director*

# CONTENTS

Page

## WITNESSES



## LETTERS, STATEMENTS, ETC., SUBMITTED FOR THE HEARING



## APPENDIX

# CONFRONTING THE IRANIAN CHALLENGE

---

## TUESDAY, MAY 8, 2018

House of Representatives,
Committee on Foreign Affairs,
*Washington, DC.*

The committee met, pursuant to notice, at 10:00 a.m., in room 2172 Rayburn House Office Building, Hon. Edward Royce (chairman of the committee) presiding.

Chairman ROYCE. All right. We will call this hearing to order.

Later today, the President will announce whether he intends to keep the United States in the Iran nuclear agreement. This is earlier than expected.

Over the past 6 months, the Trump administration has urged France and Germany and Britain to help address the full range of threats posed by the Iranian regime.

U.S. negotiators have rightly pushed for fixes to the deeply-flawed agreement, including stronger inspections, new sanctions on Iran's ballistic missiles program, and a solution to the deal's sunset problem.

Addressing these serious shortcomings is a must to keep Iran from threatening the United States and our allies with a nuclear weapon.

As I've said, this agreement's fundamental flaw is that it trades temporary restrictions for permanent sanctions relief.

Today, this committee will examine the decision before the President. As the members of this committee know, I opposed the nuclear deal and so did a bipartisan majority of the committee.

And why was this so? Because the Obama administration, in the negotiations, ditched its key goals. The deal does not shut off Iran's path to a nuclear weapon. It does not allow inspectors "anywhere, anytime, 24/7 access." It does not stop the regime's pursuit of intercontinental ballistic missiles and it gives Tehran an infusion of cash to support more of its terrorist activities around the world.

That said, I believe the best path forward at this point is to continue to fix these flaws as we enforce the hell out of the deal.

The Obama administration has put us in a tough spot. Roughly, $100 billion was given to Iran. At least $1.7 billion of that was an apparent cash ransom payment, stacked on pallets and flown, against the advice of the Justice Department and other officials, to the Iranian regime at the time when the three hostages were released.

Much of these funds have likely found their way into the hands of the Revolutionary Guard Corps. Tearing up the nuclear deal will not recover this cash. That toothpaste isn't going back into the tube.

It also won't help galvanize our allies into addressing Iran's dangerous activities that threaten us all. I fear a withdrawal would actually set back these efforts and Congress has heard nothing about an alternative.

Last week's move by Israeli Prime Minister Netanyahu to unveil Iran's secret nuclear weapons archive reminds us all what is at stake. Despite its repeated denials, Iran had a comprehensive program to design, to test, and to build a nuclear weapon.

Of course, this begs the question—what is Iran hiding today? Shouldn't we have better inspections? Remember, the deal's existing restrictions expire in the short years ahead.

The key restriction—the ability to quickly enrich uranium—begins to phase out in less than 8 years. We should be able to get an agreement with the Europeans to fix these serious flaws.

I understand we have made encouraging progress in recent weeks. If we don't have an agreement today, let's double down on diplomacy and get a deal in the weeks ahead. The Europeans need to get to yes.

And now I'll turn to our ranking member, Mr. Engel of New York, for his opening statement.

Mr. ENGEL. Thank you, Mr. Chairman. I concur with your opening statement.

To our witnesses, welcome to the Foreign Affairs Committee. We are grateful for the decades of public service that all of you collectively represent, and Jane, it's always good to see you back on Capitol Hill.

Once again, we find ourselves against a phony deadline dealing with the Iran nuclear agreement. Once again, the President has created a crisis where none exists and kept us all wondering what he's going to do.

This administration has promised a comprehensive approach for dealing with the regime in Tehran. Yet, 16 months along, the Trump administration's Iran policy seems to be do nothing until the clock runs out and make unrealistic demands of Congress or of our international partners, and up to this point, kick the can down the road a few more months.

The President has until Saturday to decide whether to continue waiving nuclear-related sanctions on Iran, though reporting this morning suggests that he will announce an end to those waivers today.

I hope he understands the stakes. If he puts those sanctions back into effect, the United States will be in violation of our obligations under the nuclear deal and trigger the deal's collapse.

The argument that the deal would continue without American participation is simply not true. There is no having it both ways, and let's be clear, President Trump would be the one who pulled the plug and undermined American credibility.

I've said more times than I can count that I opposed the deal when it was announced. I voted against it on the House floor and I continue to have doubts about the JCPOA, and I have doubts about whether it will prevent Iran from developing a nuclear weapon over the long term.

But I know for certain that pulling out of the deal now will make a nuclear-armed Iran a much more immediate threat. Some of my chief concerns with the agreement were the sunset provisions.

But those sunsets come many years in the future. What's the emergency now? Why the hysterical rush if the United States undermines the deal for sunsets that expire in 10 or 15 years would instead expire at the end of the week?

Iran would race headlong toward a bomb while keeping the cash that's been freed up over the last few years of sanctions relief.

If we want to extend the sunsets, and many of us do—and that was one of my major objections to the deal—let's work cooperatively with our allies rather than ruining any chance we have of keeping the Iranians from the bomb for a longer time.

Reimposing sanctions would also have far-reaching consequences besides terminating the JCPOA. We could find ourselves slapping serious punitive measures on our closest friends and allies.

Furthermore, it would send a terrible signal that the United States does not live up to its word and with North Korea negotiations ramping up, that is the exact wrong time to send that message.

Why would anyone negotiate with us if the minute we got a new administration or a new President they ripped up any agreement in order to get rid of it and start anew?

I think it undermines our credibility and it's the wrong message to send, and I have to note that President Trump could not have been more wrong when he said that killing the Iran deal sends the right message to North Korea.

Frankly, it sends precisely the wrong message, and that message is that the U.S. won't live up to its commitments. At the same time that the United States scuttles the deal, we would lose whatever leverage we have in trying to make the agreement stronger and addressing all of Iran's other aggressive activities.

I think there is potential for progress but it requires the United States to lead, work to bring parties back to the table, lean into new negotiations, allow the present deal to continue, and try to build on top of it.

Instead, the administration wants to sit back and say Europe needs to do the hard work or Congress needs to fix it. That's just not the way these things work.

Congress has done its part. We have given the administration all the tools it needs to crack down on Iran for its illegal ballistic missile program, its support for terrorism, its atrocious human rights record.

The White House should use these tools to craft what it promised: A comprehensive Iran strategy rather than bringing us to the brink of crisis every 3 months.

I look forward to hearing our witnesses views on this challenge. I, again, thank the chairman and concur with his remarks, and I yield back.

Chairman ROYCE. Thank you, Mr. Engel.

So this morning, I am pleased to welcome our panel. We have got distinguished guests before this committee including Ambassador Lincoln Bloomfield.

He's the chairman emeritus and distinguished fellow at the Stimson Center, and he previously served as the Assistant Secretary of State for Political and Military Affairs.

We have Mr. Stephen Rademaker who serves as senior of counsel at Covington and Burling. Previously, he served as the Assistant Secretary of State for Arms Control, before that, the Assistant Secretary of State for International Security and Nonproliferation, and before that, with this committee.

We have Jane Harman. She leads the Woodrow Wilson International Center for Scholars. Previously, she served here in the U.S. House of Representatives representing the people of California's 36th District.

And we appreciate all of them being here with us today, and without objection the witnesses' full prepared statements will be made part of the record.

Members here are going to have 5 calendar days to submit any statements or questions or any extraneous material for the record.

Obviously, the President's announcement yesterday that he'll be making an announcement on the Iran deal this afternoon and the strong expectation that he'll be exiting the agreement changes today's discussion some and it affects, certainly, for the witnesses, their written testimonies, which I've read.

I appreciate the scrambling and I am hopeful that this would be all the more reason why we should be concise here today in terms of your testimony and that way we can hear your expertise in response to our questions.

And, again, I thank you for being here to discuss these very important topics. We will start with Ambassador Bloomfield and we will ask him to please summarize your remarks if you can.

## STATEMENT OF THE HONORABLE LINCOLN P. BLOOMFIELD, JR., CHAIRMAN EMERITUS AND DISTINGUISHED FELLOW, THE STIMSON CENTER (FORMER ASSISTANT SECRETARY FOR POLITICAL MILITARY AFFAIRS, U.S. DEPARTMENT OF STATE)

Ambassador BLOOMFIELD. Thank you, Chairman Royce, Ranking Member Engel, members of the committee. Thank you for the honor of being with you this morning.

Like you, I await the President's announcement this afternoon whether he will continue to waive nuclear sanctions on Iran or withdraw the United States from the P5+1 nuclear agreement.

There are valid reasons to maintain the restraints on Iran's nuclear program under the Joint Comprehensive Plan of Action. There are also strong criticisms of the accord because it has left the world uncertain as to whether Iran still seeks to develop nuclear weapons in the future.

I find merit in both points of view and believe that the legitimate concerns of supporters and critics of the JCPOA can both be accommodated if the Congress is prepared to act.

The Iranian regime's malign activities domestically and regionally require a more effective response and the President is far from alone in his criticism of the nuclear accord.

The question is what would be a successful policy. It is not enough to be right. The U.S. needs influence, credibility, and leverage over Iran and the problems it is creating.

If the U.S. pulls out of the JCPOA, I see four serious consequences that we should hope to avoid.

First, Britain, France, and Germany, our strategic allies who've spent years negotiating this agreement, will be disappointed.

Their publics may feel as though we snubbed the best diplomatic efforts of President Macron, Chancellor Merkel, and Minister Boris Johnson.

If we end up in disputes, attempting to enforce Iran's sanctions against European companies, the West will be divided over the Iran threat.

Secondly, Iran may resume an accelerated rush to build nuclear weapons with no restraints. The head of the Atomic Energy Organization of Iran, Ali Akbar Salehi, recently said that they could resume 20 percent enrichment activities at the Fordow facility in 4 days.

Third, a nuclear arms race could break out in the Middle East. Iran's Arab neighbors across the Persian Gulf declared in 2008 that they will match any weapons capability that Iran possesses—a position reiterated in recent months.

America's pledge to maintain Israel's qualitative military edge in the region could become meaningless if Iran and its Arab neighbors are racing to build or acquire nuclear weapons.

The fourth major concern about withdrawing from the JCPOA, even when the CIA director testified last month that Iran is in compliance, is the long-term impact on Presidential diplomacy.

The day that other governments conclude that an executive agreement reached with one administration might easily be cast aside by the next President, they may insist on a treaty, requiring ratification by two-thirds of the Senate.

Not only will the House of Representatives be disempowered, but Presidential power to shape foreign policy including trade will be diminished.

That is why in my prepared statement I have suggested that the Congress amend the Iran Nuclear Agreement Review Act of 2015 so that the President no longer has to certify Iran's compliance every 90 days.

We and our allies should intensify the identification and inspection of suspicious sites. The reality is that the final milestone in the JCPOA where the International Atomic Energy Agency reaches a "broader conclusion" that Iran's nuclear activity is entirely peaceful, will never happen unless all legitimate suspicions can be put to rest.

If Iran will not extend the duration of sunset clauses in the accord, we should codify the longstanding bipartisan policy that Iran must not have nuclear weapons.

The President would leave no room for doubt by declaring this as a doctrine.

A third area of concern is Iran's ballistic missile activity. When a 2010 U.N. prohibition was lifted as part of the accord, Iran immediately began testing missiles.

Scores of missiles have been fired into Saudi Arabia from Yemen. There must be no financial dealings with any individuals, companies, banks, and organizations supporting Iran's ballistic missile program.

Five years have passed since President Obama extended the offer to Iran to pursue a path to a more respectful relationship. The nuclear deal was reached.

But Iran has shown no interest in changing its ways. For decades the clerical dictatorship has been conducting nonstop geopolitical arson, threatening regional peace and stability, international norms, and U.S. national security interests.

We, and our allies, must stand together and say, "no more."

I thank the committee and look forward to your questions.

[The prepared statement of Ambassador Bloomfield follows:]

Ambassador Lincoln P. Bloomfield, Jr.
Chairman Emeritus, Stimson Center

May 8, 2018 hearing on "Confronting the Iranian Challenge"
U.S. House of Representatives, Committee on Foreign Affairs

Chairman Royce, Ranking Member Engel, Members of the Committee, thank you for the honor of appearing before you today. This hearing takes place four days before the May 12 deadline when the President will either continue to waive nuclear sanctions on Iran or withdraw the United States from the P5+1 nuclear agreement with Iran.

The question I wish to address is "what will the world look like on May 13?" As a political centrist who has served in five prior Republican administrations, I have concluded that those who see merit in maintaining the restraints on Iran's nuclear program under the Joint Comprehensive Plan of Action, and those – including the President – who believe that Iran poses serious threats to our interests that are not addressed by the existing accord, are both right. Both points of view can be accommodated, if the Congress is prepared to act.

By May 12, the President may be prepared to recertify Iran's compliance and continue to waive nuclear sanctions on Iran. A supplemental agreement has been under discussion with Europe, which presumably would require Iran to agree. The alternative, described as a real possibility by the Secretary of State, is that the President will announce on May 12 that the US is withdrawing from the JCPOA.

I share the President's concerns about Iran but respectfully submit that withdrawal from the JCPOA is neither the only nor the best way to address them. Here is what we might see, starting on May 13, if the US pulls out of the nuclear agreement:

1. With our EU3 negotiating partners – our strategic allies – there will be disappointment, public acrimony and division, as the best diplomatic efforts of President Macron and Chancellor Merkel will appear to have been rejected in Washington.
2. Iran may resume its rapid march toward nuclear weapons and long-range delivery systems, with no JCPOA restraints. The head of the Atomic Energy Organization of Iran, Ali Akbar Salehi, recently said that if ordered by his superiors, they could resume 20 percent enrichment activities at the Fordo facility in four days.
3. A nuclear arms race could break out in the war-torn Middle East. Iran's Arab neighbors across the Persian Gulf have made clear since 2008 that they will not allow Iran to have any weapon that they do not also possess, a position reiterated in recent months. America's pledge to maintain Israel's Qualitative Military Edge in the region would be put at grave risk if Iran and any of our Arab allies embarked on a race to acquire nuclear weapons.
4. The other major consequence of our withdrawing from the JCPOA despite then-CIA Director Pompeo's testimony last month that Iran is in compliance, is the potential impact on all

future Presidents' ability to forge agreements with the rest of the world. Executive agreements are a precious currency of American power and presidential leadership; the world believes that they represent the full faith and credit of our country. The day other governments conclude that agreements reached with a current administration could easily be disavowed by a subsequent President, they may insist upon a treaty, requiring ratification by the US Senate. There are some agreements that should be treaties; but if the United States cannot transact deals with other countries without assuring a two-thirds vote in the Senate, not only will the House of Representatives be disempowered, but the power of this and future presidents over foreign policy, including trade, will be diminished.

As an alternative to the US withdrawing from the JCPOA, I recommend that the Congress consult with the President and consider amending its oversight law, the Iran Nuclear Agreement Review Act of 2015 (INARA), specifically Section II(d)(6), the provision on "compliance certification." INARA requires the President to make a certification regarding Iran's compliance with the JCPOA not later than every 90 days. That kind of legislative mechanism has been used in the past to ensure that presidents do not disregard violations by other parties to an agreement in the interest of preserving smooth relationships, and to ensure that the President – not Congress – bears political responsibility if unreported violations come to light. INARA did not provide a means to address the concerns of a President who is inclined to withdraw from the JCPOA even though Iran is complying with its terms.

The national interest would be better served by having Congress remove the certification requirement and instead require the administration to report regularly on any plausible information of possible unsafeguarded nuclear weapons-related activity. Other parties have raised questions about specific Iranian activities, and the JCPOA's Annex I, Paragraph T provides that Iran will not conduct any "activities which could contribute to the design and development of a nuclear explosive device." The reality is that the International Atomic Energy Agency (IAEA) can never reach the JCPOA milestone of a "Broader Conclusion" that Iran's nuclear activity is entirely peaceful unless all legitimate suspicions are put to rest. As a signatory to the Non-Proliferation Treaty and the NPT Additional Protocol, which it is committed to ratify under the JCPOA, Iran must cooperate fully with IAEA inspection requests.

The administration's hand will be strengthened in pressing for more comprehensive verification and compliance on Iran's nuclear program if the US and our European allies adopt a unified position, leveraging the JCPOA in a stepped-up effort to fulfill its avowed purpose and end uncertainties about Iran's undeclared activities rather than giving Iran an opening to pose as a victim and exploit differences between the US and our allies.

A second aspect of the nuclear agreement that the President has found unsatisfactory is the series of sunset clauses after which Iran will face no legal restriction on its nuclear enrichment activities, and the world will be left to rely on Tehran's assurances that all such activities will be peaceful in nature. President Obama, addressing the UN General Assembly in 2013, at the outset of the negotiations, outlined US policy toward the Middle East and North Africa, stating, "[W]e will not tolerate the development or use of weapons of mass destruction," and later adding that "we are determined to prevent Iran from developing a nuclear weapon." Mr. Obama favorably cited a religious edict from Iran's Supreme Leader against the development of a nuclear weapon; and yet, by the end of the negotiating process two years later, Iran's posture fell well short of a clear renunciation of nuclear weapons by the country's leader. Some analysts point to vulnerability in the Supreme Leader's political standing within Iran, and conclude that his negotiators were instructed to agree only to the minimum assurances necessary to achieve agreement with the P5+1.

If Iran will not unambiguously forswear nuclear weapons, now or after the sunset clauses expire, the United States can enshrine our longstanding position as a national commitment. Vice President Pence, addressing Israel's Knesset in January, already issued a "solemn promise" that the United States will "never allow Iran to acquire a nuclear weapon." The President can leave no room for doubt by reasserting this pledge as a doctrine.

A third area where the administration has expressed concern over the JCPOA is Iran's ballistic missile activity, and I share that concern. One of the UN Security Council Resolutions lifted on July 20, 2015 – six days after the P5+1 reached agreement on the JCPOA – was Resolution 1929, adopted by the Security Council in 2010, which had prohibited Iran from conducting "any activity related to ballistic missiles capable of delivering nuclear weapons." That language was modified during the nuclear talks to be non-binding under Resolution 2231. In March of 2016, just two months after the JCPOA came into effect, Iran began testing ballistic missiles capable of reaching Israel. Secretary of State Kerry suggested a new arrangement with Iran to address international concerns over Iran's missile activity. Iran's response was instructive: Foreign Minister Zarif called Secretary Kerry's complaints "baseless", while Defense Minister Dehqan called them "nonsense."

Two years later, over 100 missiles have been fired by the Houthi militia in Yemen into Saudi Arabia. The Commander of the Islamic Revolutionary Guard Corps (IRGC) has threatened missile attacks against all US forces based within 1,300 miles, meaning all US forces in the region. Exiting the JCPOA will not mitigate this threat. The US and its European allies should collaborate to trace the flow of revenues from commercial activities to the individuals, companies, banks and organizations involved in Iran's ballistic missile program, and all should be sanctioned and actively impeded within the global economy. The IRGC, which one British scholar has described as "a business conglomerate with guns," controls important segments of Iran's economy. While we and our allies improve defenses against Iranian ballistic missile threats, our governments should ensure that proposed commercial engagements with Iran will not underwrite these very threats.

Iran has been a burdensome actor dating back to the 1979 revolution. In this century alone, consider what the regime in Tehran has done to threaten the peace. It was caught secretly developing a nuclear weapons program, and then sanctioned heavily by the UN Security Council after violating its promises to EU governments and the IAEA.  It brought the world to the brink of crisis by accelerating its enrichment program.  While its diplomats kept the world's powers focused on achieving a nuclear deal, Iran's Revolutionary Guards helped the Assad regime lay waste to Syrian cities and towns, with well over 500,000 killed and millions driven into desperate exile – a massive war crime that continues today.  The Tehran regime, with its network of proxy Shi'ite militias commanded by the Qods Force, has relentlessly undermined efforts at legitimate constitutional government in Syria, Iraq and Yemen, while brutally suppressing popular aspirations at home.  Israel, Lebanon, Iraq, Yemen and Saudi Arabia are all threatened by Iranian-backed extremist non-state actors.

While we consider discrete policy questions posed by the May 12 certification deadline, Congress should bear in mind the totality of Iran's transgressions.  This clerical dictatorship has been conducting non-stop geopolitical arson, at the expense of regional peace and stability, international norms, and US national security interests.  If these norms are to survive in this century, such behavior must be actively discouraged, and its perpetrators held accountable.

When May 13 arrives, less than a week from now, my hope is that the Administration and Congress will present a unified policy response to Iran.  President Obama made a good faith offer to Iran's rulers in his 2013 UN speech, pointing in the direction of "a long road towards a different relationship, one based on mutual interests and mutual respect."  At that time, it was a reasonable overture; but today, in 2018, we have Iran's response.  They said 'yes' to the black letter requirements in the JCPOA, and 'no' to a relationship based on mutual respect.  So let us hold Iran to the requirements of the JCPOA, confirm policies that address the agreement's shortcomings, and mobilize our friends and allies to focus our efforts on curbing Iran's aggression against the Syrian people, destabilization of neighboring governments through sectarian warfare, and alarming rate of executions and other human rights abuses at home.

Letting Iran divide the US from our European allies would be a policy failure.  I am reminded of the US Army's operational doctrine that seeks to present multiple dilemmas to the adversary.  If the US and Europe can present a united front in pressing the ruling clerics in Iran to abide by the JCPOA, cease their regional aggression, and stop abusing the rights of the Iranian people, it is they who will face multiple dilemmas.

I thank the Committee for its consideration.

Chairman ROYCE. Mr. Rademaker.

## STATEMENT OF THE HONORABLE STEPHEN RADEMAKER, SENIOR OF COUNSEL, COVINGTON AND BURLING, LLP (FORMER ASSISTANT SECRETARY FOR ARMS CONTROL AND ASSISTANT SECRETARY FOR INTERNATIONAL SECURITY AND NONPROLIFERATION, U.S. DEPARTMENT OF STATE)

Mr. RADEMAKER. Thank you, Mr. Chairman and Ranking Member Engel and members of the committee. It's a pleasure to appear before you again. I thank you for the invitation.

I want to say at the outset, Mr. Chairman, I agree entirely with your opening statement. I really couldn't have put it better.

I have submitted a prepared statement. I think it makes a lot of excellent points and I urge you to read it. But since there have been some developments since I wrote the statement, I think I will depart from it and make a few additional points to those in my prepared statement.

The President, this afternoon, is going to announce his decision. According to press reports, he's going to announce that he's decided not to exercise the waiver authority that he has under existing law, going forward, and thereby allow existing U.S. sanctions required under laws passed by this committee to take effect, which I think would mark a U.S. exit from the JCPOA.

That will be an unfortunate outcome for all the reasons that Ambassador Bloomfield has identified and I am sure Congresswoman Harmon will make those points as well about the downsides to that outcome.

The point I want to make is there are basically three ways to avoid that outcome. One is for the President to change his mind. I don't think he's going to change his mind. He's drawn a line in the sand and I think today he's going to announce his determination to adhere to that line.

So we can sit here and complain that his tactics are all wrong. But I don't think he's going to listen. He's made up his mind and we know what direction he's going.

The second way to avoid it is the one that you suggested in your opening statement, Mr. Chairman, and that is for the Europeans to reach an agreement with Trump administration to fix the agreement and that—you know, I've observed this closely and I think actually the administration has made a good faith effort to negotiate with the Europeans and has come up with what I would describe as a very modest proposal.

For a man who declared that this was the worst deal ever, when you look at what he's asking from the Europeans, it's a price for keeping the United States in the deal. It's relatively modest price and, in my opinion, entirely defensible, and I will come to that in a moment.

The third way to avoid it—and it was actually I think President Trump's preferred way to keep the United States in the deal—was for Congress to pass legislation very similar to what he's asked the Europeans for.

Now, he really looked to the Senate to act on that legislation initially. There was a bill introduced by Chairman Corker and Senator Cotton, and he specifically endorsed that legislation. This was in October of last year.

He called on the Senate to pass that legislation and it was clear that if the Congress enacted that legislation he would keep the United States in the JCPOA.

That legislation stalled in the Senate. One of the reasons it stalled in the Senate was the Europeans deployed their diplomats to lobby against them and I think that's what accounts for the President's decision in January to sort of shift the onus from the Senate to the Europeans and said, if you want to work against me in the United States Congress, well, I am now going to ask something of you.

So I think that's sort of how we got to where we are today. But a third solution would be to go back to the Corker-Cotton legislation which, again, I think actually represents a defensible approach to what to do about the fundamental problem we face, which is the sunset clause.

I think even supporters of the JCPOA acknowledge that the sunset clause is a problem, that effective January 2026 Iran's ability to enrich uranium is going to go up exponentially and their ability to break out and produce nuclear weapons will become quite imminent and what do we do about that.

In my prepared statement I identify, basically, five options for addressing that problem. One of them is just to accept that idea that Iran will be able to have nuclear weapons if it's wants to after 2026.

I think that's probably the worst of the options. I don't think many people will endorse that option.

The second is to threaten to bomb them if they get close to a nuclear weapon and a lot of very respectful people have urged that option.

There was a statement here that lots of prominent foreign policy leaders signed onto in 2015 calling for that—just threatened military force if they get close to a nuclear weapon, notwithstanding that they're able, under the JCPOA, after 2026 to get close to having a nuclear weapon.

Third option, threaten them with sanctions, and that's what President Trump is calling for—threaten them with sanctions if they get close to a nuclear weapon after 2026. I mean, that's the key point. He's asking for agreement on what's going to be our policy after 2026.

So, the idea that he's asking for something that's contrary to the JCPOA is simply inaccurate—something that would put us in breach of the JCPOA is inaccurate because it is a policy statement about what would happen after 2026. Until we get to 2026, there's no argument that we've taken steps contrary to the JCPOA.

The fourth option I identify is to negotiate with the Iranians. I am here to predict that before the Trump administration is over he's going to negotiate with the Iranians.

He's getting ready next month to sit down with Kim Jong-un. I think he's going to negotiate with the Iranians.

Everything that's going on now is him laying the groundwork for a negotiation with the Iranians, I believe he's posturing. The

JCPOA is a pitiful platform from which to negotiate with the Iranians.

So he's trying to change the baseline of that negotiation. That's what's going on here and he's asking the Europeans to help him change that baseline. He's asking the Congress to help him change that baseline.

He's not getting cooperation on either of those things and that's what's leading him to make his announcement this afternoon which, as I said at the outset, is a very unfortunate development.

[The prepared statement of Mr. Rademaker follows:]

**STATEMENT OF STEPHEN G. RADEMAKER**
**Senior of Counsel, Covington & Burling LLC**

**"Confronting the Iranian Challenge"**
**Committee on Foreign Affairs**
**U.S. House of Representatives**
**May 8, 2018**

Chairman Royce, Ranking Member Engel, and Members of the Committee, I am honored to appear before you again to discuss the status of the Joint Comprehensive Plan of Action (JCPOA). I was deeply involved in the Iran nuclear issue during my service as an Assistant Secretary of State during the Bush Administration, and I have continued to follow the issue as a member of various commissions and task forces, including currently the Iran Task Force of JINSA's Gemunder Center for Defense and Strategy. I wish to stress, however, that the views I will express today are purely my own, and should not be ascribed to the Gemunder Center, the law firm for which I work, or my firm's clients.

In three previous appearances before the Committee on this issue--all prior to entry into force of the JCPOA--I expressed strong reservations about the agreement. It will not surprise you to hear that my views have not changed and I continue to believe that the JCPOA was deeply flawed.

The principal concern I have expressed on past occasions relates to the agreement's so-called sunset clauses, which provide for expiration of almost all the agreed restrictions on Iran's nuclear program after 10-15 years. I summarized my concern as follows in my testimony of July 9, 2015:

> If it is dangerous today for Iran to be able to produce a single nuclear weapon in just two or three months, why won't it be even more dangerous for them to be able to produce a much larger number of nuclear weapons in a much shorter period of time beginning just ten years from now?

I stressed that it was not just my opinion that this risk was baked into the JCPOA; even President Obama acknowledged it. In an interview with NPR on April 7, 2015, President Obama conceded that beginning by about the 13th year of the agreement, Iran's nuclear weapons breakout time will have "shrunk down almost to zero."[1]

President Trump has characterized the sunset clauses as one of three principal "flaws" of the JCPOA which he insists must be "fixed." The other two features he has identified as flaws

---

[1] https://www.npr.org/2015/04/07/397933577/transcript-president-obamas-full-npr-interview-on-iran-nuclear-deal.

are inadequacies in the agreement's inspections provisions and inadequacies in its treatment of the ballistic missile threat from Iran. He has threatened not to renew the presidential waivers of mandatory U.S. sanctions on Iran if these three flaws are not addressed, and he has called upon Congress and the governments of the United Kingdom, France and Germany (the "EU-3") to join him in adopting appropriate fixes.

Naturally I welcome President Trump's attention to the sunset clauses. For far too long, supporters of the JCPOA have blithely asserted that the agreement "cuts off all of Iran's pathways to a bomb," without including the essential qualification that this is only true for the first 10-15 years of the agreement.

But the recognition that the JCPOA has embedded within it very serious flaws does not lead to the conclusion that we should abandon the agreement today. Doing that would threaten to turn the long-term problem of the sunset clauses--a problem which will mature in January 2026, ten years after the agreement entered into force--into an immediate problem. The reality is that structure of the JCPOA frontloaded many of the benefits to Iran, while backloading most of the benefits to us. Consequently, if we abandon the agreement today, we will be unable to reclaim the benefits Iran has already received, while positioning Iran to withhold many of the future benefits it committed to provide us. I will leave it to supporters of the JCPOA to elaborate on other risks associated with this path, such as the stress it would put on our alliance relationships, the opportunities it would afford Iran to play the victim and seek to isolate the United States, and the risk of non-compliance with our secondary and financial sanctions.

It is my strong hope, therefore, that a way can be found to "fix" the JCPOA as President Trump has called for, thereby averting an immediate U.S. exit from the agreement. I believe the Trump Administration has proposed some creative ways for doing this, and I hope those proposals are seized by the EU-3 and by Congress. I will elaborate on those proposals in a moment, but first, to put the Trump Administration's approach in perspective, I want to review the options available to us for dealing with the problem of the sunset clauses.

I. Options for Dealing with the Sunset Clauses

I can imagine five possible ways of dealing with the fact that under the terms of the JCPOA, beginning in January 2026, the time required for Iran to produce nuclear weapons will begin to radically decrease, and over the following three years or so, in President Obama's words, will reduce "almost to zero."

Our options are to:

1) plan to abide by the terms of the JCPOA and simply accept this fact;

2) plan to abide by the terms of the JCPOA but not accept this fact, telling the Iranians that if they take certain steps permitted under the JCPOA we will attack them;

3) plan to abide by the terms of the JCPOA but not accept this fact, telling the Iranians that if they take certain steps permitted under the JCPOA we will re-impose sanctions on them;

4) negotiate a new agreement with Iran that eliminates the sunset clauses; or

5) abandon the JCPOA.

A careful review of these options leads, in my view, to the conclusion that our least bad option is the third, which in fact appears to be the Trump Administration's preferred course.

*Option One: Abide by the JCPOA and Accept that Iran's Nuclear Breakout Time will Reduce "Almost to Zero"*

The first option would require us to simply accept as our fate the deal that was promised to Iran in the JCPOA. In other words, taking President Obama's comments on the subject as authoritative, beginning about 13 years into the agreement (or about 10 1/2 years from today), Iran will be able to produce nuclear weapons within days, or at most a few weeks, of a decision to do so. And not just one nuclear weapon, but multiple weapons, with the number of weapons they could quickly produce growing over time. This breakout time will be shorter than can be detected by routine international inspections, meaning that we could simply wake up one day to learn that Iran now possesses a nuclear weapons arsenal.

Adopting this option might make sense if we expected Iran's government to be transformed over the course of the JCPOA into something less threatening to us and its neighbors than it has been in the past. But as of today, two years and four months into the agreement (or almost a quarter of the way to the point at which the sunset clauses begin to kick in), there is little evidence of such a transformation. Absent that, this option probably poses the greatest long-term risk of the five I've identified.

*Option Two: Abide by the JCPOA, But Threaten to Attack Iran if it Takes Certain Steps Permitted Under the JCPOA*

The second option proceeds from the recognition that the first option is unacceptable. But rather than do anything about that today, it would have us simply declare that notwithstanding what was promised to Iran under the JCPOA, we do not intend to let them come close to producing nuclear weapons, and if they do, we will use armed force to destroy their capacity to do so. To me this sounds like the most fanciful of the options, but it is the option that had the most intellectual and political firepower behind it when Congress was debating the JCPOA in 2015.

This option was recommended in the "Public Statement on U.S. Policy toward the Iran Nuclear Negotiations" issued on June 24, 2015, by the "Bipartisan Group of American Diplomats, Legislators, and Experts" convened by the Washington Institute for Near East Policy. This group included many prominent former officials of the Clinton, Bush and Obama Administrations. After expressing concern about the sunset clauses, their statement asserted:

> Most importantly, it is vital for the United States to affirm that it is U.S. policy to prevent Iran from producing sufficient fissile material for a nuclear weapon—or otherwise acquiring or building one—both during the agreement and after it expires. Precisely because Iran will be left as a nuclear threshold state (and has clearly preserved the option of becoming a nuclear weapon state), *the United States must go on record now that it is committed to using all means necessary, including military force, to prevent this. The President should declare this to be U.S. policy and Congress should formally endorse it.* (emphasis added)[2]

One of the many things the United States agreed to in the JCPOA was that there would be no restrictions on Iran's ability to produce fissile material (specifically highly enriched, weapons-grade uranium) after 15 years, and in particular no agreed limitation on the amount of such material that Iran may produce or possess. Therefore this recommendation called on the United States to effectively amend the terms of the JCPOA, not through new negotiations with Iran, but rather through the threat of unilateral military action if Iran took certain steps permitted under the JCPOA.

Personally I doubt that Iran will find this threat very credible. If America was unwilling in the days before the JCPOA to use military force against Iran when it was enriching uranium in violation of six legally binding UN Security Council resolutions, why would they believe we might in the future use military force against them for enriching uranium in a manner permissible under the JCPOA?

*Option Three: Abide by the JCPOA, But Threaten to Sanction Iran if it Takes Certain Steps Permitted Under the JCPOA*

The third option is very similar to the second, except that the threat wielded against Iran if it takes steps permitted under the JCPOA to produce excessive amounts of enriched uranium isn't a potential U.S. military strike, but rather the potential application of economic sanctions. One could argue that because the second option is capable of stopping Iran's nuclear program in its tracks, we can wait longer before applying it, thereby preserving the JCPOA for a longer time before launching military strikes that presumably would mark the end of the JCPOA. The economic sanctions of the third option, by contrast, would probably need to be applied sooner in order to have any effect. On the other hand, the third option does not have the credibility

---

[2] http://www.washingtoninstitute.org/policy-analysis/view/public-statement-on-u.s.-policy-toward-the-iran-nuclear-negotiations.

problem associated with the second option. The United States has a long history of applying economic sanctions against Iran, while the history of seeking to avoid military confrontation with Iran is at least as long.

Because the Trump Administration is pursuing a variation of the third option, I will elaborate on how this option might work in practice later in my testimony.

*Option Four: Negotiate a New Agreement that Eliminates the Sunset Clauses*

The fourth option is superficially very attractive. Instead of confrontation with Iran, it promises renewed cooperation. President Macron of France advocated this idea when he visited Washington two weeks ago. And as the debate over President Trump's proposals has unfolded during the past year, it has emerged that this is the preferred option of many other supporters of the JCPOA. Indeed, it has emerged that this was, if not the secret plan, then at least the unstated plan, of many of those who were involved in negotiating the JCPOA. There was no discussion of this idea when Congress was debating the JCPOA, however. Presumably this is because acknowledging the need for a follow-on agreement then would have raised questions whether it was really true that the JCPOA "cuts off all of Iran's pathways to a bomb."

I believe this is an option that we must take seriously, and we must also recognize that it is an option that may strongly appeal to President Trump. If he is willing to negotiate with Kim Jong Un, certainly he must be open to negotiating with Iran as well. If we are going to consider this option, however, it is important to think through where this path will likely lead.

Any negotiation proceeds from a baseline--a status quo that the negotiation seeks to alter. The baseline for negotiating the JCPOA was six binding resolutions of the UN Security Council that made Iran's ongoing uranium enrichment program illegal as a matter of international law, and a highly effective global economic embargo of Iran that was largely driven by America's secondary sanctions on Iran.[3] According to the negotiators of the JCPOA, the best deal they could cut with Iran negotiating from this baseline was the deal they got, which included restrictions on Iran's nuclear activities that sunset after 10-15 years.

Presumably the baseline for any new negotiation with Iran to eliminate the sunset clauses will be the JCPOA, which permits Iran to produce unlimited amounts of enriched uranium once the sunset clauses take effect. No one believes Iran will surrender its ability to do this as a gesture of goodwill. If Iran is going to surrender this ability, it will demand hefty compensation.

---

[3] By "secondary sanctions," I mean the threat--mandated by the Iran Sanctions Act of 1996, and a series of other laws approved by this Committee over the ensuing two decades--that the United States would impose economic sanctions on foreign persons from third countries who engaged in certain activities with Iran or with Iranian persons. Secondary sanctions are to be distinguished from "primary sanctions," which are restrictions that the United States imposes on American persons with respect to their dealings with Iran or Iranian persons.

What sort of compensation are we in a position to offer?  The most obvious candidate is relief from the primary U.S. sanctions on Iran, which are still in effect.

America's primary sanctions on Iran--the ones that prohibit Americans and American companies from dealing with Iran--were not lifted under the JCPOA because, unlike America's secondary sanctions, they were not imposed on Iran on account of its nuclear weapons program. The primary sanctions were initially imposed beginning in the 1980s on account of Iran's support for international terrorism, and they have been strengthened over time on account of Iran's continued support for terrorism, as well as other malign activities such as human rights violations against its own people, obstruction of the Middle East peace process deriving from its stated goal of wiping Israel off the map, and ballistic missile proliferation.  The position of the U.S. government going back to the Reagan Administration has been that we will only consider lifting our primary sanctions when Iran is prepared to stop supporting terrorism and doing the other things that led us to impose the primary sanctions.

It follows from this that those who want us to engage in a follow-on negotiation with Iran to supplement the nuclear-related restrictions of the JCPOA are, in reality, proposing that we consider trading our primary sanctions on Iran for additional concessions by Iran on its nuclear program.  This would be a fine idea if our only concern with Iran was its nuclear program.  But what will be left of our policy of seeking to persuade Iran to end its support for international terrorism, and its other malign activities, if we end our primary sanctions?  Are we prepared to fully rehabilitate Iran--to tell Americans and the rest of the world that they are now free to trade with Iran and otherwise treat it as a normal country--while Iran continues to act as the world's leading state sponsor of terrorism, and remains committed to the destruction of Israel?  We need to think through whether we are prepared to entertain such a deal, because this is where the path of negotiating a follow-on agreement to the JCPOA is likely to lead.

Because this is such an unsavory prospect, it may lead some to ask--and I'm thinking here in particular of President Trump--why we can't change the baseline before engaging in a new round of negotiations with Iran?  The way to change the baseline, of course, is to terminate the JCPOA and try to establish some new baseline closer to the one we had before the JCPOA was adopted.  I am deeply skeptical that this can be done, because establishing a new baseline like that will require considerable international cooperation, and I doubt much cooperation will be forthcoming if the United States has unilaterally abandoned the JCPOA.

But my real point is this: President Macron and others who are advocating new negotiations with Iran because they think that's a way of preserving the JCPOA need to be mindful that, to President Trump's ears, their arguments may come across as reasons for immediately abandoning the JCPOA.

*Option Five: Abandon the JCPOA*

The fifth option, abandoning the JCPOA, is appealing to many who originally opposed the JCPOA. And clearly it is President Trump's fallback option if the third option above proves unachievable. I have already explained why I believe this is a bad option that, if exercised unilaterally by the United States, is likely to benefit Iran more than us.

## II. Position of the Trump Administration

As I have already indicated, President Trump's current approach to the problem of the sunset clauses is a combination of options three and five above. He has called for the establishment of a mechanism that will re-impose economic sanctions on Iran if it steps up its uranium enrichment activities in a way that will shorten its nuclear weapons breakout time, and he has threatened to abandon the agreement if such a mechanism cannot be established.

To understand the Administration's position, it is useful to recall how it evolved. In October of 2017, President Trump created a great deal of suspense over whether he would make a certification provided for under the Iran Nuclear Agreement Review Act. In announcing his decision on October-, he flagged his three key concerns about the JCPOA--the sunset clauses, inspections, and missile proliferation--and called upon Congress to join him in addressing these problems, stating:

> Key House and Senate leaders are drafting legislation that would amend the Iran Nuclear Agreement Review Act to strengthen enforcement, prevent Iran from developing an inter- — this is so totally important — an intercontinental ballistic missile, and make all restrictions on Iran's nuclear activity permanent under U.S. law. So important. I support these initiatives. However, in the event we are not able to reach a solution working with Congress and our allies, then the agreement will be terminated.[4]

In January of this year, there was another round of suspense as we waited to see if President Trump would renew presidential waivers of various U.S. sanctions laws with respect to Iran. In the end he announced:

> Today, I am waiving the application of certain nuclear sanctions, but only in order to secure our European allies' agreement to fix the terrible flaws of the Iran nuclear deal. This is a last chance. In the absence of such an agreement, the United States will not again waive sanctions in order to stay in the Iran nuclear deal.[5]

Why is it that in October he placed the onus on Congress to "fix" the JCPOA, and in January he placed it instead on the EU-3? The answer appears to be that between October and January it became clear that the legislation he had endorsed--a Senate bill drafted by Senators Corker and Cotton--could not achieve the 60 votes necessary to pass the Senate. According to

---

[4] https://www.whitehouse.gov/briefings-statements/remarks-president-trump-iran-strategy/
[5] https://www.whitehouse.gov/briefings-statements/statement-president-iran-nuclear-deal/

press reports, one of the reasons the legislation stalled was because of lobbying by European diplomats in opposition to the bill.[6] President Trump therefore must have thought it was fair play to shift the onus to the EU-3.

My take-away from this history, however, is that President Trump would be satisfied either by the enactment of legislation along the lines of the Corker-Cotton bill, or by an agreement with the EU-3. In either case, the substantive elements of the "fix" would be roughly the same. They would provide for re-imposition of economic sanctions on Iran if it (1) violates its obligations to comply with inspections under the JCPOA, (2) crosses certain red lines with respect to its missile program, or (3) takes steps with respect to the production of fissile material that would shorten its nuclear weapons breakout time, including by exercising flexibilities it was afforded to enrich uranium upon expiration of the JCPOA's sunset clauses.

The first two of these features are relatively non-controversial. Few would argue that Iran should be free to violate the inspections obligations it undertook in the JCPOA. And the missile proliferation issue was not directly addressed in the JCPOA, so there is no argument that threatening sanctions over that would violate commitments that were made to Iran in that agreement. The controversial feature is the third one, and in particular the idea of threatening to sanction Iran if it takes steps permitted under the JCPOA following expiration of the sunset clauses.

Reportedly at least some of the EU-3 have objected that the mere declaration of such a policy would breach our obligations under the JCPOA. I believe this view is legally incorrect. By way of analogy, I would note that Iranian officials from President Rohani on down have repeatedly insisted that they will never allow international inspectors access to Iranian military sites, notwithstanding that they are required under the JCPOA to afford such access if the International Atomic Energy Agency (IAEA) requests it.[7] Do these policy declarations mean that Iran is today in violation of the JCPOA? I believe not, because even though Iran has declared a policy that, if acted upon, would violate the JCPOA, it has never been requested by the IAEA to permit such inspections, and therefore we don't know whether Iran would actually follow through on its declared policy. In my view, Iran will not have breached its obligations under the JCPOA until (1) the IAEA has requested access to a military site in Iran, and (2) that request has been denied by Iran.

Applying the same logic to the sunset clauses, what the Trump Administration is asking for is agreement on a policy about what will happen if, after January 2026, Iran begins to take advantage of the flexibility it will gain at that point under the terms of the JCPOA to increase its

---

[6] https://www.usnews.com/news/world/articles/2017-12-14/european-diplomacy-helps-sway-congress-to-keep-the-iran-nuclear-deal

[7] https://www.rferl.org/a/iran-dismisses-us-call-un-access-military-sites-dream-rohani-haley-iaea/28704445.html

uranium enrichment capacity. Just as with the question of international inspections of military sites in Iran, there are two levels of uncertainty here. First, it is not clear that Iran will use the flexibility the JCPOA affords it to increase its uranium enrichment capacity after January 2026. The JCPOA *permits* Iran to increase its enrichment capacity at that point, it does not *require* it to do so. Second, no matter what policy has been established (either by agreement with the EU-3 or under U.S. law), there is no certainty that sanctions will be applied if Iran takes advantage of the flexibilities afforded it by the JCPOA.

We have no idea what kind of government will be in power in the United States or any of the EU-3 after January 2026. In the case of all four countries, it is possible that the governments in power at that point will feel no more obligated to follow an agreement reached by their predecessors than President Trump feels obligated to follow the JCPOA, which was negotiated by his predecessor. And in the case of any legislation enacted into law by Congress, it presumably will include some sort of mechanism by which Congress can either approve or disapprove of the imposition of sanctions, so it is impossible to predict today what may happen under such legislation in 2026 or thereafter.

The more serious concern, therefore, is not that the establishment of such a policy today would place us in breach of the JCPOA, but rather that it might prompt Iran to withdraw from the JCPOA. Here we can only speculate about what Iran's tolerance will be for such policy declarations by us and the EU-3. But obviously it's in their interest to try to bluff us into believing that their tolerance is lower than it actually is.

Personally I believe that the JCPOA has been and will remain a very good deal for Iran, and they will not be eager to return to the pre-JCPOA days of confrontation and sanctions. So I predict they will see the establishment of such a policy as our opening move in what will inevitably be a negotiation over the shape of Iran's post-January 2026 nuclear program. As I have already indicated, it is very much in Iran's interest that such a negotiation have as its baseline the JCPOA rather than a baseline of sanctions, so I don't expect them to withdraw from the agreement over declarations today about what we intend to do after January 2026.

The final thought I want to leave you with is that, for a man who has declared the JCPOA to be the "worst deal ever," President Trump has in fact come up with relatively modest demands for keeping the United States in the deal. His tactics for persuading others to agree with his demands have not been modest, of course, but we should not allow that to obscure that, as a substantive matter, his demands appear more calculated to preserve the deal than to blow it up.

I therefore will close by reiterating what I said at the outset: it is my strong hope that agreement can be reached on some variation of what President Trump has proposed. That could take the form of either an agreement between the Trump Administration and the EU-3 (which Congress should then write into U.S. law), or agreement within Congress on a version of the Corker-Cotton bill. Either of these would be far preferable to U.S. withdrawal from the JCPOA over the objection of our allies, which appears to be where President Trump is headed if no agreement is reached.

I thank you for your attention and look forward to your questions.

———————

Chairman ROYCE. Congresswoman Jane Harman.

**STATEMENT OF THE HONORABLE JANE HARMAN, DIRECTOR, PRESIDENT, AND CHIEF EXECUTIVE OFFICER, THE WOODROW WILSON INTERNATIONAL CENTER FOR SCHOLARS (FORMER MEMBER OF CONGRESS)**

Ms. HARMAN. Thank you, Mr. Chairman, and warm greetings to so many good friends on this committee, and especially to you. We were classmates elected in the same year. Mr. Engel was a few terms ahead of us.

We served together here for nine terms and my able successor, Ted Lieu, is on the bottom row of this committee smiling at me. So I appreciate that.

But to so many of you, we were together in so many battles and I continue to care about this committee very much and wish you well as you enter your next chapter. Thank you for your really valuable service to the United States.

Like my two panelmates, I agree on where we should go. I disagree with many of you on the merits of the deal. Had I been here, I would have supported the deal.

But nonetheless, at this point, I agree strongly with you and with Mr. Engel that we should stay in the deal and proceed with many of the things that have been discussed here.

Obviously, I had prepared testimony arguing that that's not likely to happen. But I have adjusted my testimony to make a few points, some of which have already been made.

I think that, while the deal isn't perfect, if we withdraw, Iran could, and has said they will, withdraw too, notwithstanding an additional protocol which prohibits them from returning to the nuclear weapons program. I am not sure they would follow that.

Some fear that Iran might also withdraw—and you mentioned this—from the 1968 nuclear nonproliferation treaty under which 191 countries have agreed to prevent the spread of nuclear weapons and related technology.

To me, that would be a major setback and potentially provoke a nuclear arms race in the region, which has been mentioned. We would be far worse off under that scenario.

And let's not forget that there are four U.S. citizens and two green card holders in captivity now in Iran. Their chances of being released just got or just will get worse.

For sure the transformation that the Obama administration hoped for in our relationship with Iran has failed. Iran's malign behavior has not improved. It has gotten worse. We should accept that fact and address those problems with careful attention to Iranian involvement in Syria, Yemen, Lebanon, and its provocative behavior to its neighbor, Israel, our democratic ally in the region.

The results being tallied now from Sunday's Lebanese parliamentary election suggest that Hezbollah has gained seats—at least one seat—and surely gained influence in that country and that is worrisome.

There is a reason, as has been pointed out, that President Macron and Chancellor Merkel picked last week to visit the United States and that British Foreign Minister Boris Johnson visited yesterday.

Three of our closest allies urged the U.S. to stick with the JCPOA. They made clear that they are open to a four-party side agreement. The assumption would be that China and Russia, the other parties, would not join.

But the recommendations for that agreement I think we all agree on and they would make the deal better. They certainly include extending the expiration date.

There should be no expiration date requiring inspection of military sites, a moratorium on ballistic missile testing and development, and Iran ending its support of terror groups and other operations across the Middle East region.

It remains my view that addressing Iran's meddling across the Middle East won't get easier to manage without a deal.

We still lack a comprehensive strategy to address the Iranian challenge, which also evaded the Obama administration. What is our Plan B?

I think that's something this committee has a chance to address on a bipartisan basis. To me, Congress can't continue to be AWOL from the discussion of the authorization of use of military force—an AUMF.

Most of us were here when the 2001 AUMF passed. I surely voted for it, as did every member of this House except for one, and it is the basis of continued U.S. military action in the region.

My view is that it was limited in time and space and it is time for Congress to step up and address the secondary and tertiary effects of withdrawing from the Iran agreement and some of the other activities, many of them military—many of them using military technology like drones or train and assist missions in the greater Middle East, and Congress can and should do this.

I also wonder—and this was raised—whether the Trump administration has adequately considered the linkage of withdrawing here and the conversation President Trump will have, hopefully, soon with North Korea.

Obviously, the Kim regime is watching closely. By walking away from the JCPOA, we send an important message about how seriously we do or do not respect the deals to which we agree.

The contours of President Trump's decision are not yet clear. If he waives secondary sanctions against our European allies, they will likely continue to trade with Iran and that could reduce the chance that Iran withdraws from the deal.

If he doesn't waive the secondary sanctions, then he has invited, in my view, a major trade dispute with Europe, which will be amplified if he decides to impose aluminum and steel tariffs on the EU next month.

We should not underestimate the need for our allies. The Europeans are disappointed, if not dismayed, by the U.S. decision to leave the Paris Climate Accord.

They helped to construct the world order after World War II and we will pay a huge price if they move to align elsewhere.

So, in conclusion, this is a time, in my view, for Congress to step up and insist that secondary and tertiary ramifications of these issues be considered.

It is also a time for Congress to put the country first on a bipartisan basis. The stakes couldn't be higher.

Thank you, Mr. Chairman.
[The prepared statement of Ms. Harman follows:]

**THE HONORABLE JANE HARMAN**
**TESTIMONY BEFORE THE HOUSE FOREIGN AFFAIRS COMMITTEE**
**"CONFRONTING THE IRAN CHALLENGE"**
**2172 RAYBURN HOUSE OFFICE BUILDING**
**MAY 8, 2018**
**10AM**

Iran is a top US foreign policy priority, and how we handle it requires nuance.

Congress deserves substantial credit for asserting its authority over the Joint Comprehensive Plan of Action (JCPOA), by passing the Iran Nuclear Agreement Review Act, and for insisting on punishing Iran's ongoing malign behavior in the region by sending a veto-proof sanctions package to the President.

Today's hearing is about "Confronting the Iran Challenge," so my testimony starts with the JCPOA, but is intended to address the broader challenge. I'd like to make five points.

**1. Keep the Joint Comprehensive Plan of Action.**

If it ain't broke, don't fix it.

While the deal isn't perfect and was only transactional, it's better than no deal and has enormous impact on any future deal the Administration hopes to make. Many hoped the deal could be transformational, but they were wrong. We should admit it and move forward with additional strategies to deter and punish Iran's malign activity outside the so-called "four corners" of the deal. Plus, the cat's out of the bag; Iran already possesses the technological know-how.

Finally, if we withdraw from the deal, Iran could – and has said they will – withdraw too. Some fear Iran might also withdraw from the 1968 Nuclear Nonproliferation Treaty, under which 191 countries have agreed to prevent the spread of nuclear weapons and related technology. To me, that would be a major set-back, and potentially provoke an arms race in the region.

It would also strengthen the hardliners in Iran who opposed the deal and undermine any chances for a US-Iran dialogue. Plus, there are still four American citizens and two permanent US residents being held in Iranian prisons whose chances for release will worsen. This issue is personal to the Wilson Center since our colleague Dr. Haleh Esfandiari was held in solitary confinement in Evin prison in

2007. It took international effort, in which I participated as a Member of Congress, to achieve her release.

**2. There are merits to making a side agreement to improve the deal.**

There is a reason that President Macron and Chancellor Merkel picked last week to visit the United States. Two of our closest allies want to make sure that the US sticks with the JCPOA.

But they and Britain's Prime Minister Theresa May and Foreign Minister Boris Johnson have said they are open to a 4-party side agreement. (The assumption is that China and Russia – the other parties to the JCPOA – would not join.) The recommendations to improve the deal have merit: removing the expiration date, requiring inspection of military sites, a moratorium on ballistic missile testing and ending Iran's support of terror groups and operations across the Middle East region.

I hope the side agreement is being worked on now, as it would serve as the basis of President Trump's decision later this week not to decertify. Our allies in Europe are acting in good faith to produce something President Trump wants – and I found it reassuring that the President decided to delay tariffs on the EU because alienating our allies on the trade issue only complicates the Iran problem.

**3. Transformation has failed.**

Iran's malign behavior won't get easier to manage without a deal.

We must be clear-eyed that the Iranian government's strategy to expand the so-called "Shia Crescent" across the region is real, and it is in the US national interest and the interest of our democratic ally Israel and other friends in the region to limit Iranian involvement in Syria, Yemen, and Lebanon, and elsewhere. For example, while results are still being tallied, and despite low turnout, reports suggest that Hezbollah won more seats in the Lebanese Parliament.

Sadly, the US lacks a comprehensive strategy to address the Iranian challenge: we don't have a plan B for what comes after May 12 if the Administration decertifies the deal. In fairness, the Obama Administration also lacked a broader strategy. I strongly support the need for an Authorization for the Use of Military Force (AUMF) across the region to ensure we have one cohesive plan. The effort to enact an AUMF would also mean holding a public debate on the costs and benefits of a US role there.  At present, our policy is tactical and episodic, relying mostly on military technology and intelligence.

We shouldn't be shocked by new evidence Israel has produced that Iran intended to build a nuclear weapons program.  I surely never believed the Iranian program was peaceful.

### 4.  There is linkage between the JCPOA and the Democratic People's Republic of Korea (DPRK).

In announcing the Iran nuclear deal in 2015, then-President Obama said: "This deal is not built on trust.  It's built on verification."

The same must be true for any deal that we negotiate with North Korea.  And what President Trump does on Iran directly affects what he will be able to do with North Korea.  The Kim regime is watching closely.  If we walk away from the JCPOA, that's an important message to the DPRK about how seriously we do – or do not – respect the deals to which we agree.

### 5. Isolation.

In my role at the Wilson Center – voted by our peers as the best think tank in the world for regional expertise – I get to see foreign issues through a strategic lens.

In addition to Haleh Esfandiari, our experts include Robert Litwak, Aaron David Miller, Abe Denmark, and our new Korea Center Director Jean Lee who lived for two years in Pyongyang heading the Associated Press office.  My colleagues all agree that withdrawing from JCPOA will isolate the US, tank the possibility of negotiating a better deal with the DPRK and make it harder for us to work with our allies on other challenges.

We underestimate the need for our European allies at our peril.  They are disappointed if not dismayed by the US decision on the Paris Climate Accord and abandonment of multilateral trade arrangements.  They helped construct the world order after World War II, and we will pay a huge price if they move to align elsewhere.

Chairman ROYCE. Thank you very much, Jane.

Okay. So we'll focus here on some of the points that Steve Rademaker made and both of the other witnesses made.

If we go to the January 12th statement that the President made, he called for a new U.S.-EU3 supplemental agreement is what he called the addendum agreement—that would impose new multilateral sanctions if Iran develops or tests long-range missiles, thwarts inspections—these are his words—or makes progress toward a nuclear weapon, requirements that should have been in the nuclear deal in the first place and these provisions must never expire.

So these were his comments. Some of the European leaders have similar concerns. We've heard them raise those concerns with us.

So at this point, what could be done to encourage European partners to address this very important issue? I would say this is the crux of it.

The other thing that concerns me is the ballistic missile program Iran is running and what it means in terms of their transfer of ballistic missiles into Syria and into Lebanon, et cetera, et cetera, into the hands of Hezbollah and other militias.

But the key question here is just to get back to the fact that we've heard these concerns raised by the Europeans. Back in January, the President said that this kind of an addendum would be a way to resolve this.

Is there a way to get our European allies here more focused on just such a solution?

Steve, if you want to begin.

Mr. RADEMAKER. Thank you, Mr. Chairman.

The crux of the problem is that beginning January 2026, Iran, under the terms of the JCPOA, basically can have a nuclear weapon at a time of its choosing.

They will be able to produce the fissile material that they would want or that they would need to do that, and probably not just one nuclear weapon but lots of nuclear weapons and they could do it in such a short time that we wouldn't even be able to detect it before it happened.

What do you do about that? You know, a lot of leading experts said, well, not a problem—we'll just threaten to bomb them if they do that.

What President Trump has said, and what he called for in his January speech, was no, let's threaten them with economic sanctions if they do that.

And the Europeans have hesitated to agree to what he's asked for, you know, an agreement about what we would do beginning January 2026 if they use flexibility under the agreement.

Their first concern, as I understand it, is some of them say, well, this would violate the JCPOA. And the point I want to make about that is Iran has declared that they're not going to allow inspections of military sites and it's clear that the JCPOA requires them to allow inspections of military sites.

So is Iran in violation of the JCPOA by having said today, we will never do something we are required to do under the agreement?

Chairman ROYCE. Well, that's what the Ayatollah says.

Mr. RADEMAKER. Well——

Chairman ROYCE. And, of course, he makes the decision. The difficulty is that the Ayatollah took a different position, really, Steve, than his chief negotiator.

His position was, I will make the final decision—you won't be allowed on any military base.

But on that, we seem to have consensus. The Europeans agree with us on inspections. The Europeans seemingly agree with us on the ICBM aspect of it. So we can probably get there. In my view, we can get there on those two issues.

The crux of it, as you say—and I would like to hear from the other two witnesses, too—is this issue of the sunset—is there a way to phrase this, or is there a conclusion we can come to that if they roll out an aggressive nuclear weapons program at the end of the agreement that there's going to be some kind of response and, you know——

Mr. RADEMAKER. Well, I think the two reservations the Europeans have——

Chairman ROYCE. Yes.

Mr. RADEMAKER [continuing]. Is, first, there's an argument that it would be a violation of the JCPOA for them to agree to what President Trump has asked for.

Chairman ROYCE. Yes.

Mr. RADEMAKER. And on that point, I am saying just as I don't think the Iranians have violated the JCPOA yet by saying they're not going to allow these inspections.

It would not be a violation of the JCPOA for us to declare with the Europeans what our policy is going to be starting in 2026.

Chairman ROYCE. Got it. Yes.

Mr. RADEMAKER. And I think some of the Europeans are still confused and they still make the argument that, no, that would violate the agreement today for us to declare that policy that we are going to follow starting in 2026.

Chairman ROYCE. I understand.

Mr. RADEMAKER. So, satisfying them on the legal point I think is the first thing. Then the second is——

Chairman ROYCE. Let's go to Jane—yes.

Mr. RADEMAKER [continuing]. Will the Iranians withdraw from the agreement if we do that and, there, you know, look, it's in Iran's interest to bluff, right. I mean, they're going to want us to think that they would withdraw if we took that position. The question is, would they actually withdraw?

I don't think it's in their interest to go back to the days of sanctions and isolation and confrontation, which is what the reimposition of U.S. sanctions would mean.

So I think actually the risk of Iranian withdrawal is much less than some have suggested.

Chairman ROYCE. I tend to agree with you. But my time has expired. I am going to have to go to Mr. Engel for his questions.

Mr. ENGEL. Thank you, Mr. Chairman.

In his January 12th speech, President Trump said if Iran does not comply with any of these provisions, American nuclear sanctions would automatically resume.

The next waivers that are due of the 2012 NDAA sanctions which require the President to prevent foreign banks from opening accounts in the United States or impose strict limitations on existing U.S. accounts.

If those banks process payments through Iran's central bank, the law exempts those countries who significantly reduce their purchases of Iranian oil from the previous reporting period.

Ms. Harman, let me ask you this. How would this affect countries like Japan, India, South Korea, and Taiwan, which have not reduced their importation of Iranian oil?

Ms. HARMAN. Well, that's what I was trying to address in my testimony. President Trump could say that he's decertifying the deal today but he could waive the imposition of those secondary sanctions.

I surely hope he does that. I think that would be a better result. But let me also agree with Mr. Rademaker that he had better options. I mean, there's no reason to withdraw from the deal now.

There is every reason to work with our European allies who said they were willing to do it, on making the deal stronger before it expires. It's not expiring tomorrow.

And let me just add, finally, that Secretary of State Pompeo, when he was the head of the CIA, said that Iran is complying with the deal—with the four corners of the deal.

Let's understand, as the senior vice president at the Wilson Center, Rob Litwak, who's very knowledgeable about this, always says, the deal was a transaction, not a transformation.

It was a transaction to end Iran's program to pursue nuclear weapons for a finite period of time. I wish that had been infinite and I still hold out hope that that could be achieved if we took a different path.

Mr. ENGEL. Well, I would hope that it could be achieved because, as I mentioned before, that was my major objection to the JCPOA—that it didn't really prevent Iran from having a nuclear weapon, it just postponed it 15 years.

In relation to what we just mentioned, if the U.S. were to sanction companies in Asia for doing business with Iran, as we would be required to do under law, how would these sanctions affect U.S. strategy on North Korea?

Ms. HARMAN. Well, I think that this action will hurt our ability to strike a better deal—what President Trump would consider a better deal, and we all would, with North Korea because they're watching, and if they think we don't abide by the deals we make, why would we abide by a much tougher deal with them?

And I would just point out that I think it was a front page article yesterday and the Washington Post pointed out how tough it will be to administer any deal we make with North Korea.

They have a much more advanced nuclear program than Iran. Iran had zero bombs. North Korea has, depending on how you count, up to 60.

Plus, we should anticipate that they have deep tunnels all over the country which would be very hard to identify, and our intelligence on North Korea has been extremely poor up to now. We have, basically, no ground truth in North Korea.

So taking this action this afternoon I think just made the North Korea deal which, by President Trump's standards, would be—and

I agree—a crowning achievement of his presidency harder to achieve.

Mr. ENGEL. Let me ask a question about Iran's permanent presence in Syria. Let me ask either Ambassador Bloomfield or Mr. Rademaker.

How would you advise President Trump to approach the crisis in Syria after the fight against ISIS without U.S. influence and presence? Iran is likely to benefit.

Yet, the administration, in my opinion, appears to be handing Syrian territory over to the Assad regime, negotiating de-escalation zones on Israel's border that could give Iran a permanent presence in Syria, and how would a permanent Iranian presence in southern and eastern Syria affect U.S. interests in the region and affect Israel's interests in the region?

Ambassador BLOOMFIELD. Thank you, Ranking Member Engel.

The first point I would make is that the JCPOA, the nuclear agreement, dealt solely with the nuclear sector, and at a time when President Obama thought that the Iranians wanted to turn a page and reform, they didn't pay much attention to the human rights abuses at home that you mentioned and the activities in the region.

Five years have passed. As I said, it's time to look at the non-nuclear side of Iran policy. In Syria, what has occurred is nothing short of the greatest war crime of the 21st century.

Iran's Quds Force commands militia that I would estimate at 60,000 or 70,000 inside Syria made up of Shi'a militia from several countries.

The payroll comes from Tehran. The command comes from Soleimani. And he has 80,000 in Iraq as well. We've never addressed this point.

I think that what Bashar al-Assad has done cannot pass without consequences. We should be building a war crimes tribunal case against the Assad regime.

We should have had a defection program against the Syrian armed forces. We should have been making a lot of noise about Russia's reckless and promiscuous use of weapons that they give to the Syrians to bomb children and women. Over 27 hospitals were bombed when the Russians came in, along a cordon sanitaire around Damascus. Where was America's voice?

So I think it's never too late to speak up for what is right and I think the Europeans would join us in putting together a series of political measures, informational measures, and put the spotlight on Iran's aggression and let the people of Iran know where all the money's been going, because it certainly hasn't been going to the people who are protesting in Iran today.

Mr. ENGEL. Thank you.

Chairman ROYCE. We go to Ileana Ros-Lehtinen of Florida.

Ms. ROS-LEHTINEN. Thank you so much, Mr. Chairman.

Thank you to all of our panellists, all good friends.

When this administration came in, it made clear that fixing the JCPOA was going to be a top priority. We knew from the outset that there was a lot of work left to do, much of which the administration very clearly outlined in January, as we've heard, when it said this was perhaps the last chance to fix it.

The administration had simple and common sense requirements that everyone should have been able to support. But it isn't just what is in the JCPOA that the administration has rightly  said needs to be addressed.

Iran's other malign activities, which you have addressed, including its ballistic missile program, its support for terror around the globe, have largely been ignored by our P5+1 partners ever since the nuclear deal was concluded, looking the other way.

Despite years of diplomacy and despite assurances from official after official during the last administration that this would not be a problem, our European allies have been reluctant to join us in holding Iran accountable.

The administration must succeed in getting our European partners to act on the need to address Iran's malign activities.

Our European friends must agree that getting rid of sunsets that allow Iran to be a nuclear weapon state in just a few years is in all of our interests.

But if, for some reason, our partners believe that it is more important for  them to pursue their economic interest with  a  state sponsor of terror, then the President must reimpose sanctions on Iran or withdraw altogether from the accord.

Should we not get tougher enforcement and verification measures and should we not get our partners to look at the totality of the Iranian threat, then we need to start looking at what comes next.

We still have many tools at our disposal and it is clear that Iran will continue to give us every opportunity to sanction it for its illicit activity. It simply doesn't care.

No matter whether we think the JCPOA is working or not, Iran is only getting stronger in the region as it expands its influence and becomes more capable of threatening U.S. interests.

Just look at the Lebanon elections that took place a few days ago and those that are coming in Iraq this weekend.

If we keep wishing and hoping that we are going to fix the JCPOA but nobody takes any action to do so, then we'll soon be in a far worse situation than when we started, if we aren't there already.

We may need another way to ensure Iran's nuclear program is kept in check. As the chairman stated, the challenge is in how to get the Europeans on board and exert maximum pressure on the Iranian regime.

So my question then—I probably will only have time for Ambassador Bloomfield—if the President does decide to walk away from the deal—I know that Congresswoman Harman already addressed this—do you envision the need for imposing secondary sanctions?

Ambassador BLOOMFIELD. My metric of success for foreign policy, Congresswoman, would be unity among the allies. If they are on board with us on what we bring forward then we have a chance of pressuring Iran.

I want to point out that I don't think that Iran's Supreme Leader is acting from a position of strength at all. I think they are on thin ice at home. There were over 450 demonstrations last month in a country one-fourth the population of the United States.

Other Ayatollahs are sounding off against Supreme Leader Ali Khamenei. I believe a case can be made that they brought on the secret nuclear program not for military purposes but to give the Supreme Leader some status that he wasn't receiving from  the Shi'a community in the Middle East.

So they are trying to put on a revolutionary front for the people back home and it's not working.

Ms. ROS-LEHTINEN. And on the issue of secondary sanctions——

Ambassador BLOOMFIELD. So on the issue of secondary sanctions, if we lose the Europeans by going after their companies or any other companies in the world, the way to do that is to point out the suspicious sites.

We can point out any site where we have credible information, and we can insist that the rest of the world support us in demanding inspection. But it has to be based on real information.

Ms. ROS-LEHTINEN. Thank you, and thank you to our excellent panellists.

Mr. Chairman, I yield back.

Chairman ROYCE. Thank you.

Brad Sherman of California.

Mr. SHERMAN. Thank you. I want to associate myself with the opening statement of the chair and the ranking member.

A number who support the JCPOA have said that we should always regard the signature of the President of the United States as binding on our country—that the President gives  our  word  and that word is binding on us.

I would hope that Congress would reject that view. For example, this President might sign an agreement with Russia that said we will never base American soldiers in Poland or the Baltic.

Unless that is approved by Congress, it should not be regarded as binding on the American people. So I think it is legal for the President to renounce the JCPOA. It's just a terrible idea at this time.

It will meet the President's psychological needs. This agreement has the scent of Obama on it. It will meet, perhaps, his political needs. It is terrible statecraft.

The President would be doing so in order to say he wants to sanction Iran. Just a few weeks ago, a bipartisan letter was sent to the President urging him to use the existing sanctions from 2010 to sanction those who give spyware to the Iranian government to suppress its people. He has not sanctioned a single company nor has his predecessor.

It doesn't seem like the President wants to sanction Iran in order to sanction Iran. He wants to sanction Iran in order to desecrate a document signed by his predecessor.

If we are going to renounce this deal, we have to ask what rights does each party acquire if the deal is voided.

Well, Iran gets to go forward with its nuclear program. No inspectors, heavy water, unlimited centrifuges, and they can seek a return—I will get to this in a second—of the stockpile of fissile material that they shipped abroad under the deal.

What do we get? Well, we know that sanctions can change Iran's behavior. There are many reasons to sanction Iran.

Does voiding the deal allow us to impose sanctions we couldn't impose otherwise? Well, we know that voiding the deal angers Europe and Japan and makes it incredibly difficult to have effective multilateral sanctions.

But some of us—well, many of were here when John Kerry sat at that table and told us that even under the deal, adhering to the deal, we can sanction Iran in full proportion to its non-nuclear wrongdoing.

They are responsible for hundreds of thousands of deaths in Syria, tens of thousands of deaths in Yemen. They stone people to death for who they love. If they had never have thought of a nuclear program we would be coming up with every possible sanction and if we said we are doing it because of Syria and Yemen we'd have European support.

There are plenty of reasons to sanction Iran to change its behavior. Staying in the deal allows us to sanction Iran and have the hope and expectation of European and Japanese support. Voiding the deal liberates them and reduces the effectiveness of our sanctions.

I don't even know why we are talking about this. But I, believe it or not, do have a question. This deal is the good, the bad, and the ugly. Good and bad at the beginning—it gets ugly next decade.

The best part was that Iran shipped 16,000 pounds of low-enriched uranium—a little bit of mid-enriched uranium—out of the country.

They had the fissile material which, if further refined, could create several nuclear bombs. They shipped it to Russia.

Ms. Harman, would Mr. Putin—if we voided this agreement, would he entertain a request from Tehran to return that fissile material which was shipped to Russia? Would he tease us? Would he return part of it in return for more control of Syria?

How would we empower Putin, if he's sitting on 1,600 pounds of low-enriched uranium that he may or may not return to Iran?

Ms. HARMAN. First of all, let me commend Congress for something it did last year by a veto-proof margin and that was to pass the sanctions law against Russia, Iran, and North Korea that dramatically increased sanctions against all three countries.

And I think that law has been very effective and Congress did this on a bipartisan basis, so there is something to celebrate there.

What would the newly sworn-in President of Russia do? He would make mischief. I am not exactly sure how he would do it but I think that is his MO and, oh by the way, there has been a vacuum in the Middle East as U.S. leadership, in my view, has reduced that has allowed Russia to increase its power in Syria and elsewhere to our detriment.

So I think leaving the deal on a unilateral basis, if that's where this comes out, even if we do—and I hope we do—waive secondary penalties that permit Europe and Iran to keep the deal—further isolates us and that that's a mistake in terms of U.S. strategy.

Mr. SHERMAN. If the clock is accurate, I have time for one more question. But I am not sure it is.

If we simply don't enforce the secondary sanctions and all we are doing is cutting off trade with the United States, would that be sig-

nificant enough for Iran to withdraw from the deal if all they're losing is the U.S. caviar market?

Ms. HARMAN. Well, I actually don't think so. But let's understand, it does have significant effects on at least one U.S. company.
That would be Boeing, which has sold a number of airplanes to
Iran, and I think that deal would be in jeopardy and thousands of
jobs in various locations in the U.S. would be in jeopardy.

So I don't understand—I think none of us understands what the
advantage to the U.S.—and I think that's the point of your question is—from the way the administration seems to want to proceed
this afternoon.

We are all in favor of a better deal, and I think there is a path
to get a better deal.

Chairman ROYCE. We go to Chris Smith of New Jersey.

Mr. SMITH. Thank you very much, Mr. Chairman, and thank you
to this very distinguished panel for your insights.

Let me just ask you—Ambassador Bloomfield, you talked about
the payroll for the Quds Force of 60,000. Did any of that come from
sanctions relief or any of the moneys that were conveyed and do
we have an accounting yet as to how much money has actually
gone from us and the Europeans to Iran and where that money has
gone?

Secondly, maybe all of you, quickly, your assessment of
Netanyahu's disclosures—was that positive? Negative? Was it in-
sightful? Did it give you something that you had not seen before?

And then, finally, I met with Hua Qu, who's the wife of Xi Wang,
who's a Princeton graduate student. I met with him for hours.

She was practically in tears, talking about her husband, who has
now gotten a 10-year sentence for espionage—absolutely trumped
up, part of the ongoing campaign of Iran to incarcerate Americans
in order to get some kind of benefit. Because it's trumped up.

We know that Bob Levinson still remains unknown. You know,
he's 70. He's got diabetes. He needs help. All of the Americans—
and the green card members, as you mentioned, Ms. Harman—
need help.

And yet, we look at the Magnitsky Act. The last tranche in De-
cember had no Iranians on there. It seems to me we are missing
an opportunity. We've got the Countering America's Adversaries
Through Sanctions Act passed last year. There are tools.

I hope the administration uses that. I think my friend from California a moment ago made a good point. I remember hearing John
Kerry say all the other issues—human rights, you know, go all out
on the sanctioning and yet, that seemingly has not happened with
the previous administration or this one. Your thoughts on that as
well.

Ambassador BLOOMFIELD. Thank you, Congressman. So let me
start off by, first of all, making a recommendation. The first place
I ever worked in Washington was the Congressional Research Service.

I urge you to ask them to do a compendium of every law and
norm that Iran has broken since 1979, as long as they don't run
out of paper. It will be instructive to both sides.

As for the accounting for funds, this is another piece of homework that I think the Congress, on a bipartisan basis, should ask

for. Some say that up to 80 percent of the Iranian economy is controlled either by the religious foundations or, since 2005, by the paramilitary. They own the banks. They run the contracting. You can't get something big done without it going through them.

So when we talk about whether to sanction an Indian company, a European company, an American company, I think that's the wrong way to enter the conversation.

The question is, where is the money going, and if it's going to the people who are building ballistic missiles and shooting them into Saudi Arabia, if it's going into militia which are calling in air strikes on Syrian cities and towns, then that has to be an issue for us and the Europeans to sit down and say, "You can't be doing business if the money is going to these individuals, these companies, these entities, and these organizations."

I think if we take it that way, if we ask the administration to work with Congress on an intensive accounting of where the money goes, I think the sanctions issue will sort itself out.

Ms. HARMAN. Could I make a comment on human rights? Mr. Smith, you and I were in China together at the fourth U.N. Conference—I remember that—on Women, making similar points about human rights for women. It was a historic conference, and I applaud you for staying focused on that issue.

As I mentioned, there are four U.S. citizens and two green card holders presently in Iran. I think this action by the President makes it harder for us to get them out.

And this issue is really personal for the Wilson Center. One of our most famous scholars, Haleh Esfandiari, who's an Iranian American, was imprisoned in Evin Prison in 2007, and it took an international effort, in which I participated and I am sure you did, as Members of Congress, to get her out of that prison. She had gone home to visit her ailing mother.

So we have to keep an eye on this. We have to think about ways in which we can help Americans who are unfairly detained there, especially those who are ill, and it seems to me that our strategy should include that as one of the goals to achieve in the near term, and I don't think this strategy to be announced this afternoon does in an effective way.

Mr. RADEMAKER. Quickly, on the human rights issue, Congressman, let me just congratulate Congressman Sherman for recalling how Secretary Kerry and other officials of the Obama administration, at the time Congress was considering the JCPOA, emphasized that there was nothing in the JCPOA that would prevent Congress from enacting sanctions with respect to human rights violations, with respect to missile proliferation, with respect to other malign activities by Iran.

Partly in reliance on those assurances, the agreement was approved under the legislative mechanism that governed the congressional review.

But no sooner had that agreement taken effect then many officials of the Obama administration came to argue against imposing sanctions because it would be too upsetting to the Iranians and it might create problems for JCPOA implementation.

And I think that's highly regrettable and I guess—I think with Congressman Sherman I would urge Congress to listen to what the

Obama administration initially said, not what they and their alumni have said subsequently.

Chairman ROYCE. Albio Sires of New Jersey.

Mr. SIRES. Thank you, Chairman, and thank you for being here. Welcome back, Congresswoman.

I've been in this committee now the whole time I've been here—12 years—and it seems that we vote periodically on all these sanctions against Iran. But why does it seem to take so long to implement all these sanctions? I don't understand it. We just did sanctions on the generals that own sign (phonetic) business to see if we can get them to stop what they're doing.

Why does it seem that it takes so long to implement these sanctions against Iran? Anyone?

Ms. HARMAN. I think the——

Mr. SIRES. It's frustrating to me.

Ms. HARMAN [continuing]. Both people to my right are perhaps more expert on this. But I don't think it takes that long.

I actually think the sanctions have been very effective and economic sanctions as a tool of foreign policy is an asymmetric strength of the United States.

In places where we impose them we generally get results. I would say North Korea is more interested in making a deal with us because of the sanctions and Iran was more interested 5 years ago in making a deal because of the sanctions.

Was it a perfect deal? Absolutely not. But imposing sanctions and continuing to impose them on Iran's malign behavior in the region, which is permissible, is the right way to go.

Mr. SIRES. Well, I don't oppose sanctions. I just wanted the sanctions that we pass here to be implemented quicker so we can be more effective, and that's my concern, not that I am against it. I mean——

Mr. RADEMAKER. Since the subject is sanctions let me just make an observation about this. There are, basically, two types of sanctions that the United States—and by the United States I really mean Congress and by Congress I really mean this committee, because most of the Iran sanctions came out of this committee—there are two types.

There's the primary U.S. embargo, which is restrictions that we've imposed by law on American citizens, American companies with regard to their dealings with Iran, and then the secondary sanctions, which are instances where Congress has said for people not subject to U.S. jurisdictions, so for foreign companies, foreign individuals we are going to sanction you if you do something with Iran.

We don't have jurisdiction over you but we are going to deny you benefits under U.S. We are going to make your life difficult.

And, not surprisingly, those secondary sections are highly controversial when they were enacted starting in 1996 under the Iran-Libya Sanctions Act. The Europeans were very upset about that. But they're also highly effective and they had a lot to do with getting the agreement that the Obama administration was able to negotiate.

Under the JCPOA the United States was required to waive the secondary sanctions. And so when we are talking today about the

President letting sanctions come back into force we are talking about secondary sanctions.

The primary sanctions were never relaxed. The primary U.S. embargo on Iran has been in effect since the Reagan administration. It's still in effect today.

So, Congresswoman, your idea of well, maybe the President should let the snap back occur but exempt the secondary sanctions, I think basically everything that's snapping back is secondary sanctions.

So the way to avoid that is for him to exercise the waiver, which is what President Obama did and what he's done up until now, but he's saying he's not going to do that, going forward.

There really are no primary sanctions that are snapping back if the President doesn't exercise the waiver.

Ms. HARMAN. Well, just, if I may, Mr. Chairman, just respond to that. I was talking about with respect to Europeans. It's not to say that there isn't a broader point there.

But if we don't have European allies, going forward, and we have a large trade war with Europe, I worry that not only our policy toward Iran but our policy in many areas of the world will be harmed and they may move ahead and align with others and leave us isolated.

Mr. SIRES. How likely is it that all the other members of the agreement are willing to alter parts of the agreement?

Ambassador BLOOMFIELD. If I could make a comment—if we are talking about secondary sanctions that say you can't trade with Iran, that's one thing, and I think that may get us in trouble with the Europeans and others.

If, however, we look at how the Treasury Department, for example, cites individuals, entities, and what not, and we have intelligence that say, "These are the people who are doing all the malign activities," then that's the conversation we have with companies and say, "Your deal is through this front company or through this bank or through this holding company in Iran and they're the ones who our intelligence shows are paying for the Syrian operation."

So that's the conversation I would prefer.

Mr. SIRES. I was thinking when we did the financial sanctions that it seems to take forever to take effect. I am sorry. Go ahead, sir.

Mr. RADEMAKER. Well, your question was how willing will foreign—I heard your question—how willing will foreign countries be to change the deal, and I just want to stress, President Trump has not asked for anybody to change the deal.

I think, ultimately, he'd like to renegotiate it. But what he's calling for is a supplemental agreement that wouldn't change the deal but it would be a declaration of policy between us and the Europeans about what we'll do if Iran deploys missiles or tests missiles in a way that we find threatening—what we'll do if they violate their sanctions—I am sorry, their inspection obligations, and I don't think that's controversial.

And then, thirdly, with regard to the sunset clause, what our joint policy will be, starting in 2026. So he's not—he's not saying let's, you know——

Mr. SIRES. Well we don't need Iran.

Mr. RADEMAKER [continuing]. That everybody agree to—it would be let's declare a policy about what we are going to—what our countries will do, starting in 2026. But it's not a change to the JCPOA.

Mr. SIRES. Okay. I am out of time right now but thank you very much.

Chairman ROYCE. We now go to Mr. Dana Rohrabacher of California.

Mr. ROHRABACHER. Secretary Bloomfield, do I call you Secretary?

Ambassador BLOOMFIELD. No. Call me Linc.

Mr. ROHRABACHER. Okay. There you go. You went through a litany of some of the things that Iran has been doing that are very disturbing throughout the region.

Let us just note that what you're talking about costs a lot of money and what we are also talking about here is the Obama decision and as manifested in this treaty to provide $150 billion to the disposal of the Iranian regime.

And so everything that you just talked about can be traced back to a funding mechanism that we provided them.

But I would like to disagree with you on one note. You kept noting how strong Iran is. The mullah regime that controls Iran is incredibly weak, and you mentioned that as well.

You have had uprisings throughout that country, and I hate to sound like Cato the Elder. The mullah regime has to go. This is not an anti-Iranian statement. This is a pro-Iranian statement.

The people of Iran hate the mullah regime. It is corrupt. It is brutal, and all we talk about are these periphery actions when we never mention and go right to the heart of the matter, which is we should be supporting those elements in Iran that hate the regime and will replace it with a more civilized government, which they all support.

Iran is not our enemy. The mullah regime is our enemy, and while we are discussing this issue today, we should understand that. The last administration provided $150 billion to that mullah regime—not to the people of Iran, to that regime.

Let's note that my colleague mentioned the Magnitsky Act. Just so everyone will know, I support the Magnitsky Act. I didn't support calling it the Magnitsky Act because I thought that particular case had yet to be proven.

But the point is we have that power and, again, we have not designated any of the mullah regime gangsters to be punished by an act that we put forward and have passed in this Congress.

So we've been inactive in anything aimed at the mullah regime but instead broadly attacking Iran. I don't believe that's a strategy that will work.

Let me ask you—no one got around to the question about whether Netanyahu's briefing for the American people and the American government was a positive or a negative.

Maybe I could have each one of the panellists just give us a very short on their reaction to Israel.

Ambassador BLOOMFIELD. Thanks, Congressman Rohrabacher.

On the Netanyahu release of information, I think—from what I understand—I've not read it all—it demonstrates a serious program to build nuclear weapons and so then it calls into question what is the intention of the regime.

I really think the United States needs to speak with one voice and stand united. So as a centrist, let me give President Obama his due.

I think he was wrong in his assessment of Iran. In 2013, he quoted a fatwa from the Supreme Leader in front of the United Nations that they forbid nuclear weapons.

Everything that Prime Minister Netanyahu has released suggests that the Iranians were never going to give up nuclear weapons—that they would keep the knowledge in perpetuity.

So I think that there's an issue of intent and trust. Going back to what the chairman said, if I were advising President Trump, I would say whenever you get a message that comes from President Rouhani or Foreign Minister Zarif, the answer should be, I need to hear it from the Supreme Leader. He's the one and only decision maker. It's time for Iran to stop talking out of two sides of its mouth.

Going back to your final point, Congressman, about the mullah regime, I am going to quote you from Grand Ayatollah Abdollah Javadi-Amoli. He is a source of emulation.

He's a Grand Ayatollah in Qom. On April 27, he said, "Better beware that if the nation rises up the people will sweep us into the sea. Many have already fled or found a place to escape. But we have nowhere to escape to."

Mr. ROHRABACHER. And there is our solution and we've ignored that over and over again to try to get around the idea that we are recognizing the mullah regime is not Iran and we should be supporting Iran and the Iranian people.

Just really quickly, Israel's briefing—good, bad, positive? Should pay attention to it, not——

Mr. RADEMAKER. I took it as further confirmation that Iran has had a long-standing interest in acquiring nuclear weapons and in that sense to me it didn't come as news because that's been my belief for a long time. But it does underscore the need to have a serious deliberate global policy to confront the challenge we face.

Mr. ROHRABACHER. Jane?

Ms. HARMAN. I, too, always thought Iran's intention was to acquire a nuclear weapon so I wasn't surprised by it.

But I would make two other points, one on regime change. I think we should be very, very careful, given the Iraq experience, and if the people of Iran who elected their government by more than 50 percent in a four-way field want to change their government, then let them do that.

But I don't think calling for that from outside is going to improve the situation. That's my personal view.

But final point on North Korea, North——

Mr. ROHRABACHER. Unless the people who support that—the calling down the regime—end up in jail, end up having their families beaten up——

Ms. HARMAN. I think that is dreadful. That's a human rights issue and we should impose sanctions against those who do that.

Mr. ROHRABACHER. All right.

Ms. HARMAN. But on North Korea, talk about their intentions—they built 60 nuclear weapons. So let us not be naive as we do a deal with them and I am in favor of doing the right deal with North Korea.

Let us not be naive about their intentions.

Mr. ROHRABACHER. And we noted in Korea, we paid for that as well. We—again, another Democratic administration—I am sorry to sound political here—they insisted on paying money to a dictatorship in North Korea.

They used the money to what, to put us in a position where they're building nuclear weapons again, probably with the money that we gave them.

And one last thing—Netanyahu has given us an alarm bell. He's ringing the alarm bell. I am proud that our President seems to be listening to that. Looking forward to see if we act upon that alarm.

Thank you very much, Mr. Chairman.

Chairman ROYCE. Thank you, Mr. Rohrabacher.

We now go to Mr. Gerry Connolly of Virginia.

Mr. CONNOLLY. I thank the chair, and I thank the chair for holding this hearing on a day that I think is a very momentous day in terms of foreign policy in which the President is about to make a decision fraught with consequences and that could lead to the very thing we are trying to avoid—a nuclear Iran.

The fracturing of our ability to have meaningful dialogue and agreements with our allies and with our adversaries—let us remember P5 included Russia and China.

My friend from California, who chokes on criticizing a Democratic administration, nonetheless feels compelled to do so, wants to have us believe that the money released pursuant to the Iran nuclear agreement somehow was some kind of pay off for all kinds of evil things.

Primarily, it was the release of funds that had been frozen pursuant to sanctions and I got news for my friend from California—you got to have carrots and sticks if you're going to have an agreement.

If it's all carrots, I don't know what compels anybody to agree to anything, and most of that money was used to pay off huge debts the Iranian regime had incurred because of the plummeting price of oil and the effect of sanctions.

Ms. Harmon, welcome back. So listening to Mr. Rademaker, you'd think the President's just kind of making some reasonable things here. I don't think our allies are going to be all that upset.

Now, I don't know—correct me if I am wrong—I thought I saw the President of France speak before a joint session of Congress warning us not to do precisely what, apparently, President Trump is going to do this afternoon. Is my memory faulty on that?

Ms. HARMAN. I don't think so. It's also true that Chancellor Merkel made a 1-day trip from Germany and that the foreign minister of Britain came yesterday to talk to a number of people. I guess the Brits thought that he would be——

Mr. CONNOLLY. All importuning President Trump and his administration not to do it.

Ms. HARMAN. Right. But they also expressed a willingness so far as I know—and I think we are all in agreement here and I think most of the committee is—to enter into a side agreement that addresses problems that I think everyone here has with the deal.

Mr. CONNOLLY. Now, Mr. Rademaker also made the assertion that Obama administration alum—the ink was barely dry on JCPOA in terms of congressional action when they begged us not to impose sanctions on nonrelated nuclear activity.

Is it not true that there was a lot of concern up here that some people who have been overtly critical of JCPOA turned around and introduced sanctions legislation that would have in fact unravelled the agreement because they dealt indirectly or kind of almost directly with sanctions that were covered by the agreement?

Ms. HARMAN. Well, I think there was a lot of conversation about which sanctions should be imposed.

Mr. CONNOLLY. That's right.

Ms. HARMAN. There was never any doubt that sanctions against Iran's malign behavior outside the four corners of the deal, which is just a transaction to freeze Iran's nuclear program.

Mr. CONNOLLY. And forgive me. I am running out of time. But pursuant to your point, many of us turned around and voted for the comprehensive sanctions you referenced in your testimony.

Ms. HARMAN. Right.

Mr. CONNOLLY. Mr. Rademaker, let me—let me talk about compliance in the time I have left.

In the agreement—the JCPOA agreement—Iran was required to go from 19,000 centrifuges to 6,104 at the old IR1 designation. Have they complied?

Mr. RADEMAKER. So far as I am aware, they've complied with their obligations.

Mr. CONNOLLY. They have complied. On enrichment they have to go down a 3.67 percent for 15 years. Have they complied?

Mr. RADEMAKER. So far as I am aware, yes.

Mr. CONNOLLY. Stockpile—they had to reduce their stockpile of enriched uranium from 10,000 kilograms to 300 kilograms and ship it out of the country. Did they comply?

Mr. RADEMAKER. So far as I am aware, yes.

Mr. CONNOLLY. Mm-hmm. Reprocessing—they won't conduct reprocessing or reprocessing research on spent fuel, and that's indefinite. Have they complied?

Mr. RADEMAKER. So far as I know, yes.

Mr. CONNOLLY. Fordow—have they stopped enrichment at Fordow?

Mr. RADEMAKER. I believe they have.

Mr. CONNOLLY. You believe they have. On the Natanz again, they were required to limit the amount of centrifuges for research and the level of enrichment and, again, returning models to an earlier generation. Did they comply?

Mr. RADEMAKER. I can save you time. I think they've complied with all their agreements.

Mr. CONNOLLY. Well, let me just run through it because, you know——

Mr. RADEMAKER. All their obligations.

Mr. CONNOLLY [continuing]. I am trying to pay attention to your testimony here. I am trying to find flaws in their compliance.

Iraq, the plutonium production reactor, they're required to concretize their reactor and redesign and rebuild the heavy water research facility. Did they comply?

Mr. RADEMAKER. I believe they have.

Mr. CONNOLLY. Are you aware of any inspection of a nuclear facility they have not complied with?

Mr. RADEMAKER. No, I am not aware.

Mr. CONNOLLY. No. And has the IAEA and the international community certified 11 different times they are in full compliance with the agreement?

Mr. RADEMAKER. The IAEA has not found any fault with this.

Mr. CONNOLLY. And were there six Presidential certifications including with President Trump saying the same?

Mr. RADEMAKER. Yes.

Mr. CONNOLLY. Yes. I rest my case.

Chairman ROYCE. We go to Joe Wilson of South Carolina.

Mr. WILSON. Thank you very much, Chairman Ed Royce, for having this very important hearing today and thank all of the witnesses for being here.

And, Ambassador Bloomfield, to amplify further your view, Prime Minister Benjamin Netanyahu recently had a revelation of Iran's secret nuclear archive, highlighting the limits to the IAEA inspections.

The archives were apparently unknown to IAEA and other nuclear sites may have been similarly unknown.

I believe that President Donald Trump is being correct that the Iranian nuclear deal is dangerous to American families and to our allies of Israel.

Considering the information located in these archives, should the IAEA reopen its investigation into the possible nuclear dimensions—PMD—of Iran's nuclear program?

What other steps should the IAEA make to address the concerns raised by these documents hidden by the Iranian dictatorship?

Ambassador BLOOMFIELD. Thank you, Congressman.

I think we have to wait and see what details come out of the information that the prime minister of Israel has released and other information that may be available to us.

The point that I wanted to make is that, while the Iranians came to the table and said certain things can be inspected and certain things cannot be inspected, that if we find what's known as plausible information, under their language, that there may be nuclear-related activity—it may not be fissile material that's detectable through nuclear machinery—it may be designs for warheads, how to marry it with a ballistic missile, how to make the missile hit a target and to do what we've done with our ICBMs—that kind of research could be happening anywhere and more likely is under the control of the Islamic Revolutionary Guard Corps—which is a possible military dimension and would be on a military site.

So if we have any kind of plausible information, we have every right to go to the Europeans and together go to the IAEA and say, we have to inspect this.

And as I pointed out earlier, you can't get to the end point of the JCPOA—the broader conclusion at the end of several years that Iran is peaceful in intent unless you answer those questions.

So we should focus on detection, investigation, inspection, verification and be more relentless than we have been.

Mr. WILSON. And I appreciate your emphasis on verification.

And Mr. Rademaker, how would you characterize Iran's current ballistic missile capabilities and what would you expect the trajectory of their continuing missile development to be if they're not impeded by sanctions or other diplomatic measures?

At this point, what needs to be done to safeguard against the ballistic missile threat to Europe today and as they're targeting America tomorrow?

Mr. RADEMAKER. Yes. Well, Iran has a very active ballistic missile program and over time they've been increasing the range of their ballistic missiles I believe with the ultimate goal of deploying intercontinental ballistic missiles, which would be missiles that could strike the United States.

I think a critical point that needs to be made, and I think this connects back to what Prime Minister Netanyahu revealed, it makes absolutely no sense for Iran to have an ICBM if it doesn't have a nuclear weapon.

Missiles of that range—I mean, first, they're not going to be very accurate and even if they were accurate, I mean, they're not going to do that much damage.

You have ICBMs like we do to attack your adversaries with an atomic warhead, and so the fact that they're continuing to pursue these longer-range missiles I think speaks to their ultimate intentions.

They wouldn't be doing this if they did not ultimately have the intention of putting a nuclear warhead on the top of that ICBM.

Mr. WILSON. And hey, for a diplomat, I appreciate that you were very clear that ICBMs and nuclear weapons are tied together and just simply can't be separated.

And I appreciate that we've actually had bipartisan cooperation. Congressman Seth Moulton and I had an amendment to the NDAA to ask for analysis of the ICBM capabilities of Iran.

And Congresswoman Harman, thank you to have the alumni return. The current estimates that Iran has provided Hezbollah $800 million annually for their efforts, and they actually now have 150,000 missiles in southern Lebanon—a threat—and the capability of building missiles. So the threat is almost incalculable.

Following the elections last week in Lebanon, what can we do to promote a moderate influence in Lebanon?

Ms. HARMAN. Well, let me say two things.

On the missile capability of Iran, it is worrisome, and it's not just that they, over time, if this deal somehow ends, can put miniaturized warheads on top of missiles but they can also proliferate the missiles.

And let's understand that there has been proliferation between Iran and North Korea, which now has a highly advanced missile capability.

In the '90s when I served on the House Armed Services Committee, I worked with Former Senator Jon Kyl to try to block Russian technology transfers to Iran, which occurred at the time, which made their missile capability more effective.

So that's one very sad chapter in U.S. history. On this question, I am worried about Hezbollah. I mentioned the Lebanese election.

Hezbollah ran in the election. It had candidates for Parliament and it increased its seats by at least one but plus, apparently, five other seats from another party are technically under—in the Hezbollah orbit.

So not only does it have some political participation in the Lebanese government but you are correct about the missile placement in southern Lebanon and we've already seen one war between Lebanon and Israel where Hezbollah managed to lob a lot of missiles from basements of civilian houses along the border. Those were not very smart missiles. Now the missiles are smarter and have longer range. So it's very, very worrisome.

Mr. WILSON. Again, thank you all for being here today.

Chairman ROYCE. We got to Ted Deutch of Florida.

Mr. DEUTCH. Thank you, Mr. Chairman, and thanks to our witnesses for being here.

Mr. Chairman, we have three thoughtful witnesses, all of whom provided distinguished service to our country and government.

We have a chairman and ranking member of this committee and a good number of members of our committee on both sides of the aisle who are quite concerned about Iran—Iran's nuclear program and Iran's activities—destabilizing activities in the region.

And for an awful lot of us there is consensus that if the President chooses to walk away from the Iran deal—a deal that I opposed but have repeatedly said needs to be strictly enforced—the President walks away, we abdicate American leadership in all of the areas where Iran poses an immediate threat to us, to our allies, and to our security interests.

So I would just ask our witnesses, going through each of these, if I may, again, the idea being how do we retain American leadership. We can predict what Iran might do or not if the President chooses to not certify, to withdraw.

We can predict the inclinations of our allies might be. But I want to talk about what we can do to help lead those allies and if the President goes in one direction what can the rest of us—what can Congress do to continue to play that role?

So on ballistic missiles, for example, on this we heard over and over throughout the negotiation of the deal that the deal didn't cover ballistic missiles.

The President today if he wanted to could impose even tougher sanctions with respect to ballistic missiles in Iran. Isn't that right, Congresswoman Harman?

Ms. HARMAN. Yes, that's right, and should the deal have covered ballistic missiles? Of course. If they had been able to strike that deal it should have.

Should it have been term limited? No, it shouldn't have been.

Mr. DEUTCH. Right.

Ms. HARMAN. Should it have addressed Iran's other malign behavior? Yes, it should, and it still could, if this side agreement were entered into.

But can I just make one other comment?

Mr. DEUTCH. Of course.

Ms. HARMAN. And that is the need for an authorization to use military force. I think that Congress can finally construct the strategy that has been missing from everything we've been doing in the region.

The Obama administration didn't have a strategy either. They did a transaction. That's what this deal was, and other transactions as well—some correct, some less correct.

But Congress has a storied history of being able to hold hearings and get the American people engaged to understand the trade-offs in a larger U.S. role and I think that would be a huge service.

Mr. DEUTCH. Right. I think it's the most important foreign policy debate that we should be having on the floor of the House that we're not. I couldn't agree with you more.

On ballistic missiles, if we are going to be serious about ballistic missiles, don't we want our European allies to work with us to impose sanctions against Iran, Mr. Rademaker?

Mr. RADEMAKER. I think absolutely we do and, in fact, I think the agreement that the Trump administration has been trying to negotiate with the Europeans, one of the three elements was to address ballistic missiles.

Mr. DEUTCH. So—right. So let's just go through that for a second because I think there's been confusion, and I would just like to sort this out.

The fact is for the very real concerns we have about Iran's behavior, this is not just about whether the Iran deal is a good thing or a bad thing or whether Iran is complying with it or not.

The fact is that while Iran complies with the nuclear deal, they continue to hold Americans hostage. They continue to develop ballistic missiles. They continue to support terror throughout the region.

And so that deal that we've been working toward that perhaps the President may find some opportunity to push for one last time, just to be clear, doesn't violate the terms of the nuclear deal, does it?

If we give, with our European allies, a very clear signal about what will happen, as several of you have pointed out, at the end of this deal so that the sunset clause may be a sunset under the deal but we make clear with our allies that we will not allow Iran to develop nuclear weapons, something that we've said.

So why would that be a violation of the deal? It wouldn't. Ballistic missiles were not part of the deal. Why wouldn't we work with our allies to make clear what we will not accept right now in terms of threats to Europe and the United States?

And on inspections, again, if—instead of arguing back and forth over how we interpret the inspection regime that's in the deal, why wouldn't we make clear with our allies that if we believe we need to get onto a military site then we are going to work with them and if access is blocked it is Iran's fault and Iran is then in violation of the deal, from our perspective?

How are any of those unreasonable?

Mr. RADEMAKER. Congressman, I don't think any of those things are unreasonable. I think we would want to work with the Europeans on all those issues.

I do think of the three issues that we are—and here I am going to defend the Europeans, which I haven't done much of this morning—I think of the three issues that were under discussion with the Europeans, two of them were not hard, as I understand it, for the sides to reach agreement on on the issue of inspections and on the issue of ballistic missiles.

Where—the sticking had to do with how to address the sunset clause.

Mr. DEUTCH. Well—yes, Ambassador Bloomfield, I have just a second.

Ambassador BLOOMFIELD. Thank you. Sorry to go overtime.

But I believe ballistic missiles were implicated under the JCPOA agreement. There was a 2010 U.N. Security Council resolution that prohibited Iran from engaging in ballistic missile development which was lifted 6 days after the agreement was reached in June 2015 in favor of recommendatory language that was non-binding——

Mr. DEUTCH. Right.

Ambassador BLOOMFIELD [continuing]. And Iran immediately started testing missiles. And just so you know, Secretary of State Kerry said, oh, there must be a mistake here—let's have a new arrangement.

Foreign Minister Zarif called his complaints "baseless." Defense Minister Dehghan called them "nonsense." In other words, off they went.

We've been threatened by the head of the IRGC to hit all U.S. troops within 2,000 kilometres if they feel like it.

So I think we have every right to defend ourselves and to work the with Europeans to push back on their program.

Mr. DEUTCH. I greatly appreciate all our witnesses being here.

Mr. Chairman, I hope that whatever the President does today at 2 o'clock I hope he will keep in mind that the most important thing for us to do to stand up to Iran's malign behavior is to retain American leadership and I worry that he will take an action today that will weaken American leadership. That puts all of us in a weaker position.

I thank you and I yield back.

Chairman ROYCE. Thank you, Mr. Deutch.

Mr. Mike McCaul of Texas.

Mr. MCCAUL. Thank you, Mr. Chairman, and good to see the witnesses, especially my former colleague. Jane, nice to see you.

I travelled with my former colleague, Mike Pompeo, to the Middle East. Met with Netanyahu. We talked about the Shi'a Crescent—Iraq, Syria, Lebanon, coming out of Iran.

And at the time we were talking about this Iran deal we were opposed to it for a couple of reasons, all of which are being negotiated in this E3 agreement.

He and I didn't think the inspections were sufficient enough. It didn't include military sites where most likely that's where they would build a nuclear weapon.

The ICBM capability was not addressed. I asked Secretary Kerry right here why that wasn't in the deal and he simply said it just couldn't be done.

Sunset provisions have been talked about and the terror financing, from a chairman of the House Homeland Security Committee standpoint, hundreds of billions of dollars unleashed, and now look what we have.

So we are in a bit of a dilemma, I think. I think this E3 agreement was a good idea. I was hopeful it would happen. I know the sunset provisions were a problem in reaching a consensus.

But I think the question is—well, a couple. I mean, my understanding is Iran would have to agree to this as well.

Do you think if the E3 reached an agreement with the United States that Iran would join in that agreement?

Mr. RADEMAKER. So the sunset clause is a problem and I actually think the Trump administration came up with a clever way to address that problem, because implicit in your question is, would Iran ever agree to eliminate the sunset clause?

They might agree to it but not for free and I will talk about that in a moment. I talked about it in my prepared remarks.

But the Trump solution, at least what he's been trying to negotiate with the Europeans and what he asked the Congress to do is forget about the Iranians—we'll just declare what our policy  is going to be once the sunset clause kicks in.

They don't have to agree to that. We just declare this is what we are going to do, and what we are going to do is we are not going to threaten to bomb them as some people say we should threaten, although maybe—we don't necessarily not threaten to do that. But the threat we will bring to bear is the threat that we'll impose economic sanctions if they enrich uranium in a way that would get them a very short breakout capability.

No need for the Iranians to agree to that. So all it requires is the agreement of the three governments in Europe. So realistically achievable concept, I think.

Now, while we are talking about negotiations, though, I predicted in my initial statement here that before this administration is over I think President Trump probably is going to negotiate with the Iranians because he's negotiating next month with the North Koreans.

And among those who have argued that the President should not allow or should not walk away from the JCPOA, many have said, well, what he should do is negotiate the problem of the  sunset clause with Iran.

I think there will be such a negotiation but as things  stand today, we are going to have to give them something to give up on the sunset clause.

The only thing I think realistically we have to give them—well, we could write them enormous checks. Okay. We could give them a bunch of money. I don't think we are going to do that. The other—so the other thing——

Mr. MCCAUL. Well we sort of are yes. I've got a minute and a half. So——

Mr. RADEMAKER. The other thing we could give  them  is  relief from the primary embargo——

Mr. MCCAUL. Okay.

Mr. RADEMAKER [continuing]. Which is what we imposed because of their support for terrorism and so we could trade our policy—

our counterterrorism policy for concessions from them on their nuclear program.

The question I ask in my prepared statement is then what's left of our antiterrorism policy if we've given away our primary embargo in order to get additional concessions on——

Mr. McCaul. I agree, the sunset clause—I mean, that's the big sticking point. But is it better to get out entirely or do we want to extend the deadline on these negotiations rather than pull out completely?

Ms. Harman. I think that everyone shares the goal of—except, perhaps, Iran—of extending the deadline.

But the question we are all raising is what's the best way to achieve the goal, and pulling out or at least decertifying the deal today is not the best way to achieve the goal.

And I would just make one other point, which is negotiations are tough. Each party has to give up something to get to a deal. I am sure that John Kerry and others would say they wanted a stronger deal than they got.

They got the deal that they got and, as a mother of four, I know that perfection is not an option. You have got to negotiate with your own kids to get a little—to get some progress and——

Mr. McCaul. And I have five.

Just one last question—I worry too, Jane, that it will shift attention away from Iran and put it on the United States. That's one of my concerns from a foreign policy standpoint.

Finally, you talk about congressional inaction and if we can't reach this E3 agreement that perhaps Congress should take action and deal with this issue head on, whether it be with sanctions or, as you mentioned, the AUMF, and I would like to get your thoughts on that.

Ms. Harman. Well, I mentioned the AUMF a couple of times because I think Congress is AWOL and Congress should be doing this, and the 2001 AUMF that most of us who are here voted for it seems to me doesn't apply to this situation at all, and a future with a renuclearized Iran or Iran building the bomb it stopped building is one that will require some kind of military response.

So I want Congress to set the contours.

Second point, though, what is our strategy in the Middle East? What do our allies perceive our strategy is? I think it should be working, as we've all said, with Europe, who are in this deal in the first place, and hopefully with China and Russia, too, to contain nuclear developments in the region.

And if a result of this is that the Saudis or others decide to build a nuclear weapon and the Saudis could acquire technology from Pakistan, or at least that's the rumour, I don't think the Middle East becomes more stable.

So there are very serious problems, it seems to me, with pulling out, as might happen today.

Mr. McCaul. Thank you so much.

Chairman Royce. Yes. I think, for the record, in response to one our members' earlier points, the International Atomic Energy Agency is in fact currently unable to verify the provision relating to—and this is from Section T—"activities which could contribute to the design and development of a nuclear explosive device," and Russia, of course, says they have no obligation to do so.

With that said, I should go to Karen Bass of California.

Ms. BASS. Thank you. Thank you, Mr. Chair, and I want to thank all of our witnesses here today.

I guess—well, my colleague just showed me that the New York Times is now reporting that President Trump told the President of France that he is going to withdraw.

So assuming that, I just wanted to know if you three could each really paint the picture of what this looks like.

For example, Ambassador and Mr. Rademaker, how specifically would you propose to ensure that Iran is prevented from developing a nuclear weapon when it's no longer in effect, assuming that that's—again, what the New York Times is reporting is accurate? Where do we go from here is the question.

Ambassador BLOOMFIELD. Congresswoman Bass, I have already testified that I believe there are some downsides which we should avoid and whatever happens I think I want to give the President a chance to make his announcement.

It appears that there are some subtleties—that it may not be something that we can summarize in one sentence.

My hope is that whatever—the metric of success of a foreign policy is whether it is strategically credible—whether the leverage is against Iran and Iran's nuclear breakout and not against us and not dividing Republicans, Democrats, Americans, and Europeans. We should be one team. We should have a policy that goes beyond the nuclear domain to the non-nuclear domain, which everyone has acknowledged today.

So I think wherever we go from here there's a lot of past pieces that have been brought up, some with regret. We have to move forward.

And if I may—I know your time is valuable——

Ms. BASS. Yes.

Ambassador BLOOMFIELD [continuing]. I think we need a better analysis of what Iran is all about. The Supreme Leaders' followership in the Shi'a Crescent may be extremely weak.

The Supreme Leaders' readiness to come forward and negotiate with the American President——

Ms. BASS. Okay.

Ambassador BLOOMFIELD [continuing]. Or present himself may be nonexistent——

Ms. BASS. All right. I do need to move on.

Ambassador BLOOMFIELD [continuing]. So we need to analyze who we are dealing with.

Ms. BASS. Mr. Rademaker.

Mr. RADEMAKER. You ask a very good question. I do think we need to all bear in mind our President believes that, above all else, he is a negotiator. He wrote a book about "The Art of the Deal." He wrote a book about that.

Ms. BASS. Well, he hasn't demonstrated that so far, but go right ahead.

Mr. RADEMAKER. But so, I think what is going to happen this afternoon, well, technically what happens if he announces that "I am not exercising any more waivers" then on, I believe, Saturday of this week, May 12th, one of the U.S. sanctions laws will snap back into effect and it's the one called Menendez-Kirk. It was the first sort of oil sanctions—financial oil sanctions.

Well, the other sanctions don't snap back into effect until July and so I think there's a good chance what we'll hear from the President is I am letting this one law snap back into effect but the real deadline now is July, right.

Let's negotiate against a July deadline because that's when the other sanctions snap back into effect, and I hope I am right about that because what I want to see here is a negotiated solution with the Europeans. I don't want to——

Ms. BASS. Okay.

Mr. RADEMAKER [continuing]. See us go back to a sanctions realm and I just hope that——

Ms. BASS. Okay.

Mr. RADEMAKER [continuing]. The President's psychology probably lends itself to that.

Ms. BASS. And Congresswoman, perhaps you could continue to explain that. I mean, if the sanctions snap back that impacts Europe, doesn't it?

Ms. HARMAN. Well, yes. I am hoping that there won't be a snap back and my colleagues might ask then what will he be announcing.

He'll be announcing the fact that he's unhappy with the deal, which we've heard before, but that he's waiving its worst effects.

And I am still hoping that what this entire committee seems to want—surely I do and I think all of us want—is a side deal gets negotiated with our European partners and that becomes the basis over time of improving the deal.

But I think it would be a big mistake to blow up the deal totally or blow up the U.S. role in the deal. Even if Iran stays in the deal that would have the effect of isolating us.

Ms. BASS. So how do you pull out of the deal and then put it back together and then have a side deal? I don't—you know what I mean?

Ms. HARMAN. Well, I think it takes a lot of legal maneuvering. But I think there is possibly a way to thread the needle and I am sure he's looking at it in terms of stating his intention, not recertifying it. Remember, he said he didn't want to recertify it last time. But having its effects be minimized against our European partners, perhaps not our Asian partners—I think that would not be the wisest course but perhaps that's the way he will go.

Starting a major trade war right now with Europe and possibly in June, as I mentioned in my testimony, also allowing these proposed tariffs on steel and aluminum to be in effect against Europe is a huge, I think, mistake.

Mr. RADEMAKER. I think—to the extent you're asking a technical question—if he allows the sanctions to be reimposed how does he get out from under that if he later changes his mind—and actually the answer to that is very simply he will still have the waiver authority.

So if sanctions could snap back into effect but if an acceptable deal is negotiated at some point thereafter he can just exercise the waiver authority again and restore the situation that exists today.

Ms. Bass. Yeah. I don't know——

Mr. Rademaker. I will be surprised if this afternoon he doesn't—I would be surprised if he closes the door to negotiations.

I would expect him to say, I am doing this because we haven't gotten satisfaction in the negotiations but I am still here. I still want to negotiate. I still hope—you know, and——

Ms. Bass. And so the problem is none of us know what he's going to do from day to day. That's the problem.

Thank you.

Chairman Royce. We go to Lee Zeldin of New York.

Mr. Zeldin. Well, thank you, Mr. Chairman. Thank you to all the witnesses for your service

Mr. Rademaker, one of the comments that you made with the questioning with Mr. Connolly you said you believe—your understanding is that Iran has complied with all of their obligations.

We are aware, though, that the IAEA has found them twice to be over their heavy water limit, right?

Mr. Rademaker. That's correct. That was a problem that the Obama administration solved by buying excess heavy water from Iran.

Mr. Zeldin. Yes. So that was one of the violations, I just want to correct the record on a few different items, and I don't want to embarrass anyone here but just a few components that are important to point out with regards to Iran's compliance or lack thereof.

So Annex 1 Paragraph 61 of the JCPOA states, "Iran will only engage in production of centrifuges to meet the enrichment R&D requirements."

Iran has acquired more than the necessary amount of IR8 centrifuge rotor assemblies for R&D purposes with 16 times more capacity than the IR1 to enrich uranium.

With regards to exceeding IR6 centrifuge allowance, as part of the JCPOA an enrichment research and development plan was submitted to the IAEA that permitted, roughly, 10 IR6 centrifuges.

Iran has assembled 13 to 15 IR6 centrifuges, which should have been limited or destroyed under the plan.

With regard to conducting mechanical testing of advanced centrifuges in violation of the JCPOA Iran has exploited the conditions governing the quality assurance of advanced centrifuges to conduct mechanical testing of advanced centrifuges.

With regards to refusing IAEA access to military sites, under Annex 1 Paragraph 76 of the JCPOA, the IAEA can request access to military locations such as Parchin to verify compliance.

The Iranian regime has made crystal clear before, during, and after the negotiations that they will not allow access to any of their military sites.

With regards to possessing chemically manmade particles of natural uranium, in September 2015 Iranian officials granted limited access to the IAEA inspectors at the Parchin facility.

The environmental samples revealed chemically manmade particles of natural uranium. The IAEA did not pursue an explanation.

The IAEA director general stated that the agency wants Iran to fully implement the JCPOA which, by implication, covers Section T, as was referenced by our chairman of Annex 1 of the JCPOA, which prohibits any activities that could contribute to the development of the—of a nuclear explosive device.

It should be noted that when we went to Parchin and we noticed that there were some particles consistent with what they are not allowed to have, they did not allow further access to their site following that.

So we were not actually allowed to get our inspectors there to follow up on those—on those particles.

So I just wanted to correct the record on those few things.

Mr. Chair, I have 2 minutes. Do you want me to yield to you for the remainder?

Chairman ROYCE. No. No, that's quite all right. Go ahead with your line of questioning if you wish.

Mr. ZELDIN. Okay. So I would just add a couple of quick points then. One is I am deeply troubled by the activities of the Secretary of State—Former Secretary of State John Kerry. He's no longer the Secretary of State and his activities right now really are deeply troubling.

He wasn't very good when he was the Secretary of State. He shouldn't be acting like one still today. There was some back and forth earlier with regards to ransom and the payment that was made, and that was money that was owed to the Iranians.

But the part that was left out was that that money had to be given to the Iranians in cash simultaneously with the release of American hostages.

So, that part—again, just completing the record from an earlier exchange—was left out. This was money that was owed. This wasn't ransom. In order to release the hostages, money in cold hard cash had to arrive in pallets simultaneously in order to release the hostages.

I have 30 seconds left. Anyone—did you want to respond, Mr. Rademaker, to the earlier point?

Mr. RADEMAKER. Well, since I was the one who was sort of dragged into conceding that Iran is in compliance with the JCPOA, let me just observe, I think you pointed to some potential technical violations.

But big picture—my view has always been that the JCPOA is such a great deal for Iran that they would have to be out of their minds to cheat on it.

Now, that doesn't mean we shouldn't scrutinize them because they've cheated on plenty of agreements in the past—they might be tempted to cheat on this one.

But rationally—the rational thing for them to do is comply fully, comply scrupulously, and then reap the dividend of the sunset clauses starting in about the tenth year because then they'll be able to have everything they want. So why jeopardize that by cheating to gain some small advantage today when they get enormous advantages by operation of time?

And, we are almost 2½ years into the agreement at this point. So we are a quarter of the way to them being able to reap all the benefits.

So the closer we get to the 10 years, which is January 2026, the less incentive they'll have to cheat because they just wait a little bit more time and they won't have to cheat.

Mr. ZELDIN. Yes. Important points. Thank you for mentioning all of them. I think, in a way, Iran can't help themselves but to cheat and to test the limits and see what they can get away with.

But I just—I need to correct the record because it was—it has been stated way before today's hearing by many people that Iran has not violated the letter of the JCPOA and we could debate over how significant one might think all the violations are. But it's just inaccurate to say Iran has not violated the letter of the JCPOA. There actually have been many different violations of the letter.

Thank you, Mr. Chairman.

Chairman ROYCE. We go now to Bill Keating of Massachusetts.

Mr. KEATING. Thank you, Mr. Chairman.

You know, most of the attention today will go with the President's decision to pull out of the agreement. I wish there was more attention on this hearing because I do believe Congress has a role. This committee has a role, a major role, and if you listen to this morning's testimony you'd see, generally speaking, bipartisan agreement that pulling out is the wrong approach and has consequences that are going to be deleterious and there's room to go and I just want to talk about a few of those things.

Now, people cavalierly just say, well, 8 years and they can do whatever they want. Well, that's not true under the agreement. There are limitations that are for 10 years, 15 years, 25 years, and permanent limitations. Those are in the agreement.

Now, the sunset issue is one that there are some restrictions on this, going forward, limitations on this. And our approach to this and to the inspections issue, which Secretary Mattis said, in his own words, "pretty robust verification"—his words.

So the inspection process is enforcing these limitations under the sunset. We should take a policy with our allies of extremely and aggressively pushing inspections, certifications.

That is already at our disposal if we work together and work hard, and if they're violating it that coalition coming together can make adjustments themselves and that's where we should be going with this.

Now, there are issues with the ballistic missile program and the activities of the Quds Force—the malign activities of the Quds Force.

But within that coalition—and independently we can deal with that—but working with the coalition we can be more effective dealing with those issues.

And here's my point—by pulling out—and I've talked to the leaders in the other countries—there's no surprise here—they're staying in, our allies, and the division that that's going to cause is just going to undercut our ability to do what I just said—aggressively enforce what's there. Stand together and make sure that's being done. That's being ripped apart with that.

Can you comment on the real harmful effect of us being able to enforce this strongly as a coalition being undercut by this pulling away from the agreement?

Ms. HARMAN. Well, I am not sure if that's addressed to me but I totally agree with the comments and I think I've tried to make the point several different ways.

You also made a point that I hadn't mentioned yet, which is that Former Secretary of Energy Ernie Moniz, who was a key negotiator here—he was the actual nuclear scientist in the room—claims that a number of provisions in the deal are permanent.

For example, he says that because of the way we track plutonium production Iran will never be able to—never, not in 10 years, not in 15 years, not in 25 years—ever be able to produce a plutonium weapon which is a—certainly, a form of nuclear weapon that has devastating consequences and that some other provisions, as you said, last more than 10 years. So——

Mr. KEATING. And I would agree with you, Secretary Moniz, and any scientist will tell you that we are concerned about inspections——

Ms. HARMAN. Right.

Mr. KEATING [continuing]. And the 28-day delay. That material is around for a lot longer than we are going to be here and it's totally detectable. So that delay is not going to hurt our ability to do it.

That's in there, in the agreement as well. So there are things in here that we can deal with and work together with and maybe expand the issues that surround it. But we have to do it with that coalition that was so successful. We can't do it alone.

Ms. HARMAN. And—right. One of the real selling points of the deal was the P5+1—the fact that it's the permanent members of the U.N. Security Council plus Germany, and that includes China and Russia.

And the fact that we could get to a deal even if not a perfect deal—I made the point before——

Mr. KEATING. I am in my last minute so I am sorry—I apologize to interrupt but you just mentioned something else that's important.

Right now in Russia Putin has had a pretty good week with his ceremony being reinstalled as their leader. This really completes his week.

This division with the West is exactly what Russia has been gearing toward and continues to undercut a coalition that's been there since the end of World War II that's brought more peace and prosperity to this world than any other time period. He's trying to undercut it quickly.

Putin must be having a pretty good laugh about this happening right now, don't you think?

Ms. HARMAN. Yes. I was asked what are his intentions and I said to make mischief.

Ambassador BLOOMFIELD. If I could answer, Congressman, since I am from Massachusetts—I think one of the deficits here is that we didn't really focus on Russia's interest in the P5+1 negotiation.

Here he was sitting on our side of the table and somehow the arms embargo got lifted for conventional weapons. I used to be in charge of arms sales in the State Department.

And suddenly old deals were being carried out, deliveries were being made, and now he's got a new market for the Russian arms industry. We've never really commented on that and that's a bit of cynicism.

They weren't exactly in the same place strategically that we were with the Western Europeans. So that's a problem.

I also think, though, that it's important to give a political explanation for what was happening at the negotiating table on the Iranian side. We've been talking about what they can do in 8 years, 6 years, et cetera.

That's true. But what they really did was to transition from being an illegal outlaw nuclear rogue state to being a legal nuclear power.

That was the big thing. It already happened. They became fully legal in 2015-2016. So I personally—and I go back to the things I've said before—don't look at this regime in Tehran as sort of planning for 2026.

They're trying to get through 2018, and I think that knowledge, that sensibility, could help us come together on a policy on Iran that puts leverage and pressure on them to back off and looks at their vulnerabilities.

Mr. KEATING. Well, thank you. I yield back.

Chairman ROYCE. Okay. We are going to go to Ann Wagner of Missouri.

Mrs. WAGNER. Thank you, Mr. Chairman, for this timely hearing. I want to also thank the witnesses for their service.

When the last administration signed its very flawed nuclear deal with Iran, many hoped that the economic incentives would entice Iran to leave its destabilizing violent agenda behind and to join the community of responsible nations.

I, quite frankly, never shared that optimism. Nearly 3 years later, Iran's behavior remains deeply disturbing. Iran's support for Assad and for terrorist groups throughout the region compromises U.S. interests and, frankly, the security of our allies.

It is absolutely critical that the United States use its strength and its economic clout to hold Iran accountable for its proxy army of terrorist groups and extremists militias.

Ambassador Bloomfield, U.S. policy makers see factionalism in Iranian domestic politics as kind of a ray of hope. But you have criticized Washington's long-standing kind of naivete in this regard and I agree. Wishful thinking has impaired policy makers' ability to assess the Iranian threat with clear eyes.

Dissenting factions within Iran have yet to succeed in modifying the regime's behavior abroad, it seems. However, that's not to say that meaningful change can never happen.

Can you assess here briefly the long-term possibilities for internal reforms in Iran, please?

Ambassador BLOOMFIELD. I will. Thank you very much, and I agree with all of your comments, Congresswoman.

There are several countries in this world which are one-party authoritarian states—Russia, China, Syria, North Korea, Iran.

These are circles of power that have similarities, even though the culture is different. They never intend to lose power.

This regime has been in power for nearly 39 years. It's the same people. Some of them become hardliners and then 10 years later they're reformists.

I am not saying that they are all identical drones. No human race produces people who agree on everything. We fight about politics in Washington. They fight about politics in Tehran.

But if the people push hard enough and complain about the economic deprivation, the lack of rights, the abuse, the executions—more than 50 percent of the executions in the Middle East are Iranian executions—the Tier 3 trafficking in persons, how they're hanging people from ropes for trafficking drugs but we are catching IRGC 18-wheelers in Europe with drugs.

Mrs. WAGNER. Right.

Ambassador BLOOMFIELD. And so there's so much that could be said about what they've done. If this ever catches up to them, not one of the reformists—not one of the moderates—can walk down the street and not be told, "You were part of the 39-year reign of terror."

So I think they all know that. Everything that they do is to stay in power, and I think when you start with that piece of wisdom, and consider the JCPOA, they came to the table maybe because of economic duress.

But let me just say that even if we hadn't given them all that money, they have huge oil reserves. They share one of the largest gas fields on the planet.

They have tens of billions—upwards of 100 billion, probably, in the religious foundations. The issue is not whether we are giving them the money, although I know it upsets people. The issue is, they have the money.

They're just not spending it on the people, and that's a fight between the Iranian people, 80 million of them, and this circle of clerics that has held power for 39 years.

Mrs. WAGNER. I appreciate that perspective very much and appreciate it being in the record.

Mr. Rademaker, I haven't seen the preannouncements of the President's announcement but let's just say that the President does decide to either reimpose sanctions or walk away from the Iranian deal at this point.

How can we use it to our advantage to perhaps strengthen his hand in the North Korean denuclearisation talks? Do you see any way, shape, or form in doing that?

Mr. RADEMAKER. That's an interesting question. The conventional wisdom—and I think we've heard it expressed here today—is that walking away from the JCPOA makes it harder to strike a deal with North Korea because they'll assume that President Trump can't be trusted to honor commitments that the United States makes.

I think there's a lot to be said for that argument. But I think that's probably not President Trump's analysis.

I think probably his analysis is the opposite—that it will be a signal of strength and determination that he sends to the North Koreans—that by walking away from a deal that didn't adequately address the nuclear threat from Iran he's showing them that he's going to settle for something that's inadequate.

Now, I think a lot of people would disagree that that's the effect but I do think actually——

Mrs. WAGNER. I think it is. I will say this. I believe that it is America's strength. I believe it is the maximum pressure campaign.

I spent some time in the Korean Peninsula and on the China-North Korea border and I do believe that our strength, the sanctions package, has brought players to the table, especially Kim Jong-un, and it'll be interesting to see what dynamic this has I think going forward.

So Ms. Harman, please—Congresswoman.

Ms. HARMAN. If I just might add to that, though, as Linc Bloomfield just said, regime survival is hugely important to the Iranian regime.

I think regime survival is just as important to the Kim regime in North Korea, and they've been in power for 70 years and presided over the most atrocious human rights abuses and so forth. We all agree with that.

So if they're interested in regime survival, why would they voluntarily give up a pretty highly-developed nuclear industry to a goal of denuclearization? Why——

Mrs. WAGNER. Because their people are suffering. Their people are starving. Their people are under such oppression from both the human rights and economic standpoint.

I believe that's why—certainly why North Korea has come to the table.

Ambassador Bloomfield, do you agree? No? Good.

Ms. Harman, please. You can finish up.

Ms. HARMAN. Just to respond, I think the regime is responsible for a lot of that starvation——

Mrs. WAGNER. It is.

Ms. HARMAN [continuing]. And deprivation of rights, and I think if it gives up its nuclear weapons and allows for an entry into the normal world by North Korea, it risks its survival. I am not making that case. I don't want that to turn out to the be true.

But I am saying from the perspective of the Kim regime, I think they will be reluctant to now restore or provide for the first times rights to their people because they could easily be overthrown.

Mrs. WAGNER. Thank you for your perspective.

Mr. Chairman, I appreciate the time and I will yield back.

Chairman ROYCE. Okay. We go to David Cicilline of Rhode Island.

Mr. CICILLINE. Thank you, Mr. Chairman. Thank you to our witnesses.

I think the President's behavior in this context is dangerous. It is undermining the security of the United States and our interests around the world.

His antics demonstrate a tremendous lack of understanding of the implications of withdrawing from this agreement  and  using this deal as a rhetorical wedge for political gain and playing a will he, won't he game of certification is a distraction from the very serious issues including keeping our ally, Israel, safe, combatting terrorism in the region, having a strategy for success in Syria, and opposing Iran's various malign activities throughout the region.

And while we are dithering about certification of sanctions waivers and bullying our European allies, the Iranians, in concert with

Russia and Syria, have set up a sphere of influence that stretches from Tehran to Damascus.

The New York Times is now reporting that the President is actually going to reimpose all the sanctions, and so this hope that somehow he was going to be a great negotiator—we were just going to add to the deal, Mr. Rademaker, doesn't seem very likely.

And it's not the language the President has been using. He's been talking about it being the worst deal in the world and he's going to fix it, and what he's going to do is undermine our ability to really provide leadership in responding to Iranian aggression around the world.

Many of us saw making certain that nuclear weapons were off the table would actually enable the United States to lead an effort to really respond to the malign behavior of the Iranians in various parts of the world and their effort to really enlarge their sphere of influence.

All of that is thrown out now. It's hard to imagine how anyone will be willing to work with the United States in developing a real strategy to do that when we aren't keep our word in this international agreement.

So I know, Congresswoman, you have mentioned this in your testimony. We are in the middle of this discussion about denuclearizing the Korean Peninsula.

If you're Kim Jong-un and you're watching this and thinking oh, here was an international agreement led by the United States in which they promised to give up their nuclear program in exchange for certain things.

Everyone admits they have complied with the agreement. This idea of, like, well, maybe not with the spirit—it's just not true. Everyone who has reviewed it said they are in compliance. When you have an agreement, you have terms. You either comply with them or you don't.

And so I just wonder what it means in terms of our ability to actually resolve another very difficult question on the Korean Peninsula when we have some challenges now with our partnership with our allies as a result of this walk away coupled with some credibility as to whether we'll keep our word.

So, Congresswoman, I would love your thoughts on that.

Ms. HARMAN. I think that if President Trump can reach a strong deal with the North Koreans he will deserve enormous credit. That will be huge, as he discusses it, and I give him credit all the time for making North Korea the first focus of his foreign policy.

So I am all for a strong deal with the North Koreans and I am all for the conversation which will take place soon somewhere.

But I do think, as you said, that decertifying this deal or at least in some way pulling away from this deal is going to make it harder to negotiate with the North Koreans. I just made that point.

I think that the Kim regime in North Korea has regime survival as its first tenet—not helping its people but regime survival—and it figures that by doing a deal that will welcome it back into the community of nations it will enhance its ability to survive.

I also think a second goal is somehow unifying the Korean Peninsula, which could be achieved because South and North Korea are finally talking to each other and may finally end the Korean War, which has never had a formal end.

So those goals are achievable but by watching what happens today they may be fading farther away on the horizon.

Mr. CICILLINE. Thank you.

The other question is there are mechanisms that are available to the administration today under the Global Magnitsky Act as well as CAATSA.

Now, whether any of the witnesses know how many Iranians are being sanctioned under those two provisions currently?

You know, this idea of, like, we already have these vehicles and is the administration making use of them. Does anyone know? Are there any?

Ambassador BLOOMFIELD. I don't know the answer to that. It appears that we don't know but——

Mr. CICILLINE. All right.

Ambassador BLOOMFIELD [continuing]. But I would say that our military leaders have constantly said that all tools of national power should be mobilized in support of U.S. policies and I am not sure we are quite there yet.

Mr. CICILLINE. Yeah. Thank you.

And finally, I know there has been some discussion about what I would put in quotes as "evidence" submitted by Prime Minister Netanyahu last week about the prior intentions of the Iranians some—almost two decades ago.

It was clear to everyone who was studying that deal that that was information that was known to U.S. intelligence agencies, known to negotiators.

In fact, if we didn't have some believe that they were intending to do that we wouldn't need the JCPOA. So this was not any surprise to anybody on the panel, I take it?

Ambassador BLOOMFIELD. Can I respond to that, please?

Mr. CICILLINE. Sure.

Ambassador BLOOMFIELD. First of all, I am a centrist and I like bipartisanship. And in that spirit, if we go back to the beginning of the nuclear talks, I am not as hard on President Obama for seeing an opening when the Iranians reached out to see if we could reduce their nuclear threat and maybe move relations to a better place.

He went before the United Nations and he not only said we want to negotiate a nuclear agreement but in 2013 the President also said we would like to see if we can follow a path to better understanding between the two countries.

What we have is the answer from Iran. It's 2018. We have a different President. We have the nuclear agreement. That was done.

But the rest of it—Iran's intentions, Iran's nature—has been revolutionary. It has been to export and foment trouble, to try to destroy the ability of the Syrians to get to a constitutional government.

With the Iraqis that we bled and died for to have a constitutional government, they have committed sectarian warfare to undermine that, because the next stop is Tehran. That's my view.

So I think it's appropriate for this President to say, "Wait a minute—this isn't enough." Now, I don't know what he's going to say about the JCPOA.

My own view is that it only talks about part of the problem. If there's no restraint, we have a crisis. If there is restraint, let's move to the rest of it, and that's what I've tried to explain today.

Mr. CICILLINE. Thank you.

Congresswoman.

Ms. HARMAN. If I could just add a comment to that. I applaud the statement, but let's remember what the deal was. It was a transaction to get Iran to stop its development of nuclear weapons for a finite period of time. That's it.

It was not a transformation of the relationship. That was aspirational and, sadly, those aspirations did not come to pass.

But my view is we should still keep the transaction and negotiate a stronger transaction, meanwhile, working with our allies to keep the whole area more stable through an authorization to use military force, which Congress could enact.

Mr. CICILLINE. Thank you very much.

Thank you, Mr. Chairman.

Chairman ROYCE. Mr. Tom Garrett of Virginia.

Mr. GARRETT. Thank you, Mr. Chairman, and I want to say to the three honorable and distinguished members of the panel that I apologize in advance.

As a junior member, I am going to covetously guard my 5 minutes. I won't get six or seven.

So I want to start, Ms. Harman, with a comment that you made. If the people—and I quote verbatim—"If the people of Iran who elected their government by more than 50 percent in a four-way field want to change their government let them do it."

Are you implying that there are free and fair elections in Iran?

Ms. HARMAN. No.

Mr. GARRETT. Okay.

Ms. HARMAN. But I am implying that——

Mr. GARRETT. I am going to covetous—I am not trying to be rude and I respect your immense service to this body. But I want to be clear, because the Iranians watch these hearings, right.

So the Guardians Council approves individuals who wish to run for office in Iran and, as an example, 496 individuals wanted to run for President in 2009. Four were approved. So it's not so simple—regime change—as winning an election, and I don't want to—and, again, not meant to be disrespectful.

I want to read from the comments of my colleague, who I think was nearly prescient when he wrote in 2015 the following: Now, under U.S.—now as the law—under U.S. law the only thing that's binding on the U.S. is a tree that's designed as a treaty. So it says it's a treaty submitted to the Senate for ratification, it gets two-thirds positive vote. This deal is not a treaty. It has no standing under U.S. law except as a handshake from the President.

I continue from my colleague—the Vienna Convention of Law of Treaties provides a hierarchy of agreements.

This deal is not a ratified treaty. It's not an unratified treaty. It's not an executive legislative agreement. It's the lowest form of international handshake.

So I continue from my same colleague: You can be sure that Iran will violate this agreement or not, based on whether it's in their interest, whether they think they'll get caught. No one around the Ayatollah will say no, no, that would be a violation of international law.

And so I want to thank my colleague, Mr. Sherman, because I think he's really been sort of omniscient as it relates to foreseeing what happens.

Mr. Rademaker, do we know, to a metaphysical certainty, that Iran is in compliance with the terms of the JCPOA?

Mr. RADEMAKER. No, I don't think we——

Mr. GARRETT. And, again, not trying to be rude. I got a finite amount of time.

And we don't know that because military sites are off limits to inspections, correct?

Mr. RADEMAKER. They've declared that they will be off sites. There's been no request to inspect military——

Mr. GARRETT. And if there is an inspection request, how much time do the Iranians have to prepare?

Mr. RADEMAKER. I am not sure, but they would have—they would have some time. The bigger question, though, is are there other sites that we don't know about at all that we don't to inspect.

Mr. GARRETT. That would be the next question. And initially contemplated was 24 days to prepare. My colleague, Mr. Sherman, very humorously but I think accurately said, "I could clean out my garage in 24 days."

And so, again, I commend him for sort of being—having foresight.

Let me ask you this. Linc—because that's what you said somebody to call you—is a nuclear-armed Iran consistent with the rhetoric from the mullahs an existential threat to entities in the region as well as the nation state of Israel and, depending upon the delivery mechanism, an existential threat to millions and millions of people in the United States?

Ambassador BLOOMFIELD. As a technical physical matter, of course it is.

Mr. GARRETT. Okay.

Ambassador BLOOMFIELD. I've already explained why I think they need it for political reasons more than military reasons.

Mr. GARRETT. I understand, again, and I know I am sort of limiting these questions but I am limited in time.

Does Iran have a documented history, Mr. Rademaker, of violating international agreements?

Mr. RADEMAKER. Well, when it came to—in the nuclear area they have a long history of deception and cheating on their international obligations with regard to nuclear safeguards.

Mr. GARRETT. And my good friend and colleague, Mr. Engel, pointed out that the—well over $100 million—in previous statements that there are well over $100 million that we released to Iran would go to fund activities that the Iranians have engaged in for perpetuity to include Hamas, Hezbollah wreaking havoc in the region and globally.

Can anyone on the panel, just for my own sort of intellectual curiosity, name a single terrorist entity other than Hezbollah, which

is a wholly-owned subsidiary of the Iranian government which has
the dubious distinction of having murdered people on every single
inhabited continent? Can anybody, or is Hezbollah—are the Iranians the only ones?

Australia? South America? So I suppose, in conclusion, Mr.
Rademaker, would you feel better about this agreement as was in-
dicated by my colleague, Ms. Frankel, as well as Mr. Deutch and
Mr. Sires in 2015, if the inspection were more robust?

Mr. RADEMAKER. Certainly.

Mr. GARRETT. Would each of you feel better about this agreement
if the fungible moneys weren't freed to Iran that have historically
gone to fund radical elements that murder people across the globe,
quite literally, like Hamas, Hezbollah, et cetera? Ms. Harman, I
saw you reaching for the button.

Ms. HARMAN. Of course I would.

Mr. GARRETT. And so if we can maintain some agreement and
yet get a stronger agreement as it relates to things like ballistic
missile technology that would, in the estimation of all folks on the
panel, be a step in the right direction?

Ms. HARMAN. Absolutely, but the question we raised is whether
the President's anticipated action this afternoon helps or hinders
that goal.

Mr. GARRETT. Well, Ms. Harman, I will wrap up.

Again, with complete respect for everybody on the panel, I would
read from my friend and colleague, Mr. Deutch, who wrote in 2015,
"Many of my colleagues are trying to turn this into a  partisan
fight." People of good faith can disagree. Honestly,  they  should
stop.

We do not know what the actions of the President will be circa
2:00 p.m. this afternoon. I will be completely candid in speaking for
or against them once I understand what they are.

But in the meantime, trying to score political points,  I  think
you'd all agree, is a bad idea and we can do a little bit better with
this thing that has been referred to as a deal and an agreement
but not a treaty and it is indeed within our legal purview to at-
tempt to do so by virtue of the nature of the underlying agreement.

Is that not correct, ma'am? Anybody?

Ms. HARMAN. Yes, it's correct, and this committee, on a bipartisan basis has stated a general position, which I certainly would
commend and I commended at the outset of my testimony the bipartisanship, the long history of it—of this committee. I think it's
an exemplary part of the House.

Mr. GARRETT. The only thing I would submit, and not to poke at
you at all, is that we should not judge what the President is going
to say before he said it.

That's all. Thank you, Mr. Chairman.

Chairman ROYCE. Thank you. Thank you very much, Mr. Garrett.

Lois Frankel from Florida.

Ms. FRANKEL. Thank you, Mr. Chair.

Mr. Schneider, thank you for still being here because it's usually
just myself and the chairman at the end.

All right. So there is a benefit to lasting a couple of hours of the hearing because there's always something happening, which is I got a news alert that Russia opens the door to rework Iran deal.

Apparently, their foreign minister just said that they're interested in the French proposal. I don't know what that means. I just thought I would bring that out. Maybe I will ask a question about it.

So, listen, here's the point that we all agree. First off, thank you for being here. I know we all agree, everybody, that Iran should never get a nuclear weapon, and there's no conflict between believing that and those of us who agree that the deal was flawed.

I personally did not like the deal because I thought Iran's dangerous actions were left unaddressed, the sunset clauses and so forth—all these things that are still pressing.

With that said, I think we need to fix, not nix, and I—as much as I disagree with this President on almost everything, I really— even though he's going to today say he's going to impose sanctions—apparently he's going to impose all the sanctions back—I really—I find it hard to believe that he's really going to do that. Maybe it's diplomatic chess.

But here's my question. I hope that's what it is. From a practical point of view, first, I wanted to ask you this. Let's say he imposes sanctions—reimposes them.

How long does it take to get them—the consequences, which I think he's trying to get to, which is a better deal—so from a practical effect, what does the administration have to do to make the imposition of the sanctions actually work? What are the next steps?

Ambassador BLOOMFIELD. It may be, Congresswoman, that they've already done some homework on this and so it's very hard to predict. I think the bureaucracy will work very hard and probably very well.

The effect will be immediate. The rial—the Iranian currency—is very weak right now and dropping. A news flash at 2 o'clock from Washington that the President is unsatisfied with this regime's behavior will resonate throughout the country and out of fear people just not knowing what the sanctions will do will have a negative effect on their currency.

Ms. FRANKEL. Okay. So what do you think is the risk of them starting up the—to try to have a nuclear weapon that actually is effective?

Ambassador BLOOMFIELD. Could I just, for the record, point out that in January, before the Israeli Knesset, Vice President Pence made a "solemn promise" that the United States will never allow Iran to have a nuclear weapon. That's a check we have written— this administration has written.

That's why in my testimony I suggested perhaps the President should enshrine it as a doctrine. We hope that Iran will agree not to develop a nuclear weapon under these arrangements.

But if they do, this is a promise that the Obama administration also made. This is bipartisan. We have said they will never have the bomb.

Well, we have to hold to that. That's a red line.

Ms. FRANKEL. Ms. Harman, 1 second before you answer the question, okay, let me—okay, answer that question because I do have another one. Go ahead.

Ms. HARMAN. Well, 1 think it has always been U.S. policy at least as long as we've worried about Iran. First it was U.S. policy that they could not—should not—it certainly was my view, get intercontinental ballistic missile technology and transfer it to others. They did get that. That's the point.

But I think the Obama agreement, as we have discussed, was transactional and it should—if it remains in effect in some effect, that would be a positive.

What I was going to say is that one of the downsides of an announcement that we are leaving the deal is the reaction of our allies.

Let's understand this deal is much more effective because we had three European countries plus China and Russia in the deal, and what happens next? Maybe some new mischief from Russia is going to be fascinating. But we probably will not be in the driver's seat.

Ms. FRANKEL. What do you think the actions will be by Iran and do you think there's any possibility that they would agree to a new agreement—a new add-on?

Mr. RADEMAKER. So I don't even know yet what the President's going to announce at 2 o'clock. So it's hard for me to——

Ms. FRANKEL. I am assuming he's going to announce the worst. I don't know whether he'll follow through but——

Mr. RADEMAKER. Assuming the United States reimposes sanctions that's a breach by the United States of its obligations under the JCPOA, then as a legal matter Iran, if it wants to walk away from its obligations, it's entitled to do so. Whether they will do that or not, I don't know.

They may benefit politically by playing the aggrieved party and continue to comply and asking for compensation in other areas. That would be a shrewd clever strategy on their part.

Would they be open to a new negotiation? You know, I think absolutely, and the—you should read my prepared statement on this. I talk about what negotiations on a follow-on agreement would look like.

From today's baseline, if the baseline is the JCPOA and we are asking Iran to make additional concessions, they're going to naturally say, well, what are you prepared to give us in exchange and what I point out in my testimony is the main thing we have to give them in exchange is relaxation or elimination of our primary embargo.

In other words, we promise, okay, we are going to stop treating you like an economic pariah. American companies, American individuals will be able to trade with Iran in the future just like any other country.

That would be a good deal for Iran. But then my question, which I asked in my prepared statement, is what's left of our counter terrorism policy because——

Ms. FRANKEL. Right.

Mr. RADEMAKER [continuing]. We imposed those sanctions to stop them from supporting Hezbollah, to get them to back off from their commitment to destroy Israel.

And if we decide to rehabilitate them, turn them into a normal nation because they make some additional concessions in the nu-clear area, what's left of our efforts to stop them from supporting terrorism?

Ms. FRANKEL. Right, and——

Mr. RADEMAKER. And that's the question——

Ms. FRANKEL [continuing]. And you can't—how can you renego-tiate—can't in 5 minutes? It doesn't take 5 minutes to get a deal. We need to try to stop their terrorism, and I am just worried what they're going to do in the meantime.

Chairman ROYCE. All right. We go now to Mr. Brad Schneider of Illinois.

Mr. SCHNEIDER. Thank you, and I want to thank the chairman and the ranking member for having this hearing and, like my col-leagues before, I associate myself with your remarks.

I want to thank the witnesses both for staying here and sharing your perspectives but also for your past service to our country.

About eight witnesses ago—because we now have instant alerts on our watches—New York Times reported that the President is going to withdraw, moments ago, Haaretz is quoting, France is de-nying that President Trump told Macron that they're going to with-draw.

So I think we are at a point where we have absolutely clarity from this. But I think where there is clarity and, among the com-mittee and on both sides as well as the witnesses, we talked about that there's agreement Iran should never ever have a nuclear weapon.

That was true before the JCPOA. It is true for the terms of the JCPOA and I believe it should be true after elements of the JCPOA sunset.

Ambassador Bloomfield, you, in your written testimony, talked about the fact that the United States has the ability—and I believe it should and I felt this way before the JCPOA—we should make clear that we will never ever allow Iran to have a nuclear weap-on—not now, not during the terms of this agreement, not after-wards.

Is there anything preventing the President or, for that matter, Congress from making that statement?

Ambassador BLOOMFIELD. I am not aware of any nor was I aware of any when President Carter called the defense of the Persian Gulf a vital interest to the United States. These are things that Presi-dents do.

Mr. SCHNEIDER. And I think that would be true long, long into the future.

Earlier, there was talk about compliance—Iran's compliance with the nuclear arrangement and that there weren't flaws in the com-pliance.

I just want to make clear—my issues with Iran's compliance or flaws at the moment it's when there are sunsets. The flaws, I be-lieve, are within the deal. And I believe that, like any deal, there are inherent risks in the JCPOA. I believe there are gaps in the JCPOA and, particularly, with sunsets and some of the other issues there are flaws.

But I also think it's important that we recognize that the JCPOA has bought us time. In fact, Gadi Eizenkot, in January 2016—the chief of staff of the Israel Defense Forces—said that we need to use this time to develop a strategy and create the leverage.

We've pushed Iran back for a year for up to 15 years. That's a good thing. But we have to keep Iran back and permanently away from a nuclear weapon.

Does pulling out of the deal now create any more leverage? I will look to you, Mr. Rademaker, if you can touch on that.

Mr. RADEMAKER. President Trump may calculate that negotiating some follow-on agreement from the baseline of the JCPOA is a losing proposition because the only thing we have to give them is additional sanctions relief of our primary embargo and he doesn't want to do that.

So he wants to change the baseline. That's sort of how I interpret what he's been doing.

Can I comment on this related issue, though?

Mr. SCHNEIDER. Yes.

Mr. RADEMAKER. Declaring a policy that we are not going to allow Iran to have a nuclear weapon—I mean, look, that sounds right. Let's declare it.

But you need to answer the question, what are you going to do about it, okay. If they—and I think the implication of this declaration is we are going to attack them, okay—that we will attack Iran if it gets close to having a nuclear weapon. I am fine with that declaration. Okay.

But what President Trump has been asking for, what he asked the Congress to legislate and what he asked the Europeans to agree to was not join us in threatening to attack Iran.

He said join us in threatening to impose sanctions on Iran if they get close to having a nuclear weapon.

The Europeans said, oh, no, no, that might upset the Iranians— we can't do that. Legislation to do that stalled in the Senate——

Mr. SCHNEIDER. If I can——

Mr. RADEMAKER [continuing]. And I guess, you know, if you're going to declare this policy you got to put some teeth in it and if——

Mr. SCHNEIDER. Fair enough.

Mr. RADEMAKER [continuing]. The only teeth are the threaten to— we are going to threaten to attack them, that's safe—threatening to oppose sanctions on them, that's dangerous, I don't——

Mr. SCHNEIDER. Well, let me reclaim my time because in your testimony you talked about we either accept it or reject it. I don't believe we should accept the flaws. I think there are things we can do to close the gaps, reduce the risks, and try to fix the flaws.

But I don't think it's either-or. I think there's a sequence, and I think what we need to do is say how do we put pressure on Iran to change its behaviors—change its behaviors around ICBMs, change its behaviors around their efforts to expand within the region—change its behaviors on support of terror and human rights, and that should be a full-throated across-the-board pressure.

But behind that there also, I believe, has to be ways to box Iran in and the credible threat of military action has to be a part of that.

We said before all options—all options have to be on the table. But most importantly, within that, I believe, we need to create strategic options—create leverage for the United States to force Iran to change its goals, to understand that we are not going to accept a nuclear Iran and that means working with our allies, maintaining the relationship and, as my colleague, Mr. Deutch, said earlier, ensuring that American leadership is indispensable and enforced.

I am sorry.

Ms. HARMAN. Well, if I could just enthusiastically embrace that, that's why I think Congress has to enact an authorization to use military force for the region, which would identify the trade-offs and how to create a strategy for United States leadership that puts maximum pressure not just on Iran—and by the way, we can curb its malign behavior outside the contours of the deal and we should be done more—but against other parities in the region who are engaged in nefarious activities in any country where they are.

And we should dispel this notion that the U.S. is leaving the region and retreating from our responsibilities, that we have developed since the end of World War II with allies that have created an order in the world that's valuable and we should try to maintain.

Mr. SCHNEIDER. I think our leadership is more important now than ever.

Mr. Rademaker, do you have a response——

Mr. RADEMAKER. Just a concluding thought. Authorization for use of military force—fine idea. What President Trump asked for, I would say—asked the Senate to do—would properly be characterized as an authorization to impose economic sanctions, and the Senate wouldn't do it. So——

Mr. SCHNEIDER. Well, that's why—I think there's a sequence of things. We need to be able to apply the pressure, have the critical threat, and work to build the strategy long-term well beyond 2025, well beyond 2030, to make sure Iran never gets a nuclear weapon.

Ms. HARMAN. The American people deserve a voice in this. They have to understand what the trade-offs are in terms of resources and loss of life, and they haven't been included in the conversation the way they could be if Congress, on a bipartisan basis, led by this committee, would debate seriously and, hopefully, help pass an authorization to use military force.

Ambassador BLOOMFIELD. Well, if I could just offer a final thought. I support what you're saying about strong American leadership, about authorization for use of military force, about having a debate, about doing the right thing on the nuclear issue.

I also feel that we need a much stronger view of the vulnerability of the Iranian regime, and I think what you're saying is we need to understand their legitimacy problems, their economic mismanagement problems, their criminal record, the accountability for all of the things that they've done not only to us but to the rest of the region and the world.

We've never held them to account. We've never even had a full accounting of what this regime has done. If we do that, we will see a very weak and isolated group of leaders who are on thin ice and who are trying to make a lot of noise and hold up bright shiny objects in order to gain a little bit of legitimacy and buy some time.

I think if we do that, we can put together a comprehensive strategy that uses the wisdom that my two panelists have offered. I support much of their wisdom of what they put forward on the nuclear side.

But let's also have a comprehensive policy that says once and for all that this malign actor needs to be pushed back in the box.

Chairman ROYCE. And, Ambassador, we'll—we will be—Brad, you and I, Ambassador, this committee will be further engaged in that discussion with you and with all three of our witnesses today.

I really want to thank you for your testimony and we thank the members also for your questions.

So in about an hour the President will let us know his decision with respect to sanctions and, by extension, the nuclear deal, and we'll see what he has to say and go from there.

And this committee will stay engaged. But for now, we stand adjourned and thank you, again.

[Whereupon, at 12:39 p.m., the committee was adjourned.]

# A P P E N D I X

Material Submitted for the Record

# FULL COMMITTEE HEARING NOTICE
# COMMITTEE ON FOREIGN AFFAIRS
## U.S. HOUSE OF REPRESENTATIVES
### WASHINGTON, DC 20515-6128

**Edward R. Royce (R-CA), Chairman**

May 8, 2018

**TO:  MEMBERS OF THE COMMITTEE ON FOREIGN AFFAIRS**

You are respectfully requested to attend an OPEN hearing of the Committee on Foreign Affairs to be held in Room 2172 of the Rayburn House Office Building (and available live on the Committee website at http://www.ForeignAffairs.house.gov):

**DATE:**  Tuesday, May 8, 2018

**TIME:**  10:00 a.m.

**SUBJECT:**  Confronting the Iranian Challenge

**WITNESSES:**  The Honorable Lincoln P. Bloomfield, Jr.
Chairman Emeritus and Distinguished Fellow
The Stimson Center
(*Former Assistant Secretary for Political Military Affairs, U.S. Department of State*)

The Honorable Stephen Rademaker
Senior of Counsel
Covington and Burling, LLP
(*Former Assistant Secretary for Arms Control and Assistant Secretary for International Security and Nonproliferation, U.S. Department of State*)

The Honorable Jane Harman
Director, President, and Chief Executive Officer
The Woodrow Wilson International Center for Scholars
(*Former Member of Congress*)

### By Direction of the Chairman

*The Committee on Foreign Affairs seeks to make its facilities accessible to persons with disabilities. If you are in need of special accommodations, please call 202/225-5021 at least four business days in advance of the event, whenever practicable. Questions with regard to special accommodations in general (including availability of Committee materials in alternative formats and assistive listening devices) may be directed to the Committee.*

# COMMITTEE ON FOREIGN AFFAIRS
## MINUTES OF FULL COMMITTEE HEARING

Day __Tuesday__ Date __05/08/2018__ Room __2172__

Starting Time __10:05AM__ Ending Time __12:39PM__

Recesses __0__ (___ to ___) (___ to ___) (___ to ___) (___ to ___) (___ to ___) (___ to ___)

**Presiding Member(s)**

*Chairman Edward R. Royce*

*Check all of the following that apply:*

Open Session ☑  
Executive (closed) Session ☐  
Televised ☑

Electronically Recorded (taped) ☑  
Stenographic Record ☑

**TITLE OF HEARING:**

*Confronting the Iranian Challenge*

**COMMITTEE MEMBERS PRESENT:**

*See attached.*

**NON-COMMITTEE MEMBERS PRESENT:**

*N/A*

**HEARING WITNESSES: Same as meeting notice attached? Yes ☑ No ☐**
*(If "no", please list below and include title, agency, department, or organization.)*

**STATEMENTS FOR THE RECORD:** *(List any statements submitted for the record.)*

**Statement for the Record - Representative Gerry Connolly**

*Question for the Record - Representative Dina Titus*

TIME SCHEDULED TO RECONVENE __________  
or  
TIME ADJOURNED __12:39PM__

Full Committee Hearing Coordinator

# HOUSE COMMITTEE ON FOREIGN AFFAIRS
## *FULL COMMITTEE HEARING*

| PRESENT | MEMBER |
|---|---|
| X | Edward R. Royce, CA |
| X | Christopher H. Smith, NJ |
| X | Ileana Ros-Lehtinen, FL |
| X | Dana Rohrabacher, CA |
| X | Steve Chabot, OH |
| X | Joe Wilson, SC |
| X | Michael T. McCaul, TX |
|  | Ted Poe, TX |
|  | Darrell Issa, CA |
|  | Tom Marino, PA |
| X | Mo Brooks, AL |
|  | Paul Cook, CA |
| X | Scott Perry, PA |
| X | Ron DeSantis, FL |
|  | Mark Meadows, NC |
| X | Ted Yoho, FL |
| X | Adam Kinzinger, IL |
| X | Lee Zeldin, NY |
|  | Dan Donovan, NY |
|  | James F. Sensenbrenner, Jr., WI |
| X | Ann Wagner, MO |
|  | Brian J. Mast, FL |
| X | Brian K. Fitzpatrick, PA |
|  | Francis Rooney, FL |
| X | Thomas A. Garrett, Jr., VA |
| X | John Curtis, UT |
|  |  |
|  |  |
|  |  |

| PRESENT | MEMBER |
|---|---|
| X | Eliot L. Engel, NY |
| X | Brad Sherman, CA |
|  | Gregory W. Meeks, NY |
| X | Albio Sires, NJ |
| X | Gerald E. Connolly, VA |
| X | Theodore E. Deutch, FL |
| X | Karen Bass, CA |
| X | William Keating, MA |
| X | David Cicilline, RI |
| X | Ami Bera, CA |
| X | Lois Frankel, FL |
|  | Tulsi Gabbard, HI |
| X | Joaquin Castro, TX |
| X | Robin Kelly, IL |
|  | Brendan Boyle, PA |
| X | Dina Titus, NV |
|  | Norma Torres, CA |
| X | Brad Schneider, IL |
|  | Tom Suozzi, NY |
|  | Adriano Espaillat, NY |
| X | Ted Lieu, CA |

**Statement for the Record**
*Submitted by Mr. Connolly of Virginia*

Following months of destabilizing threats and spurious claims about the Iran nuclear deal, President Trump is widely expected to announce this afternoon that he will not continue to waive key sanctions pursuant to the Joint Comprehensive Plan of Action (JCPOA). Such an action would constitute a violation of the agreement and lead to its inevitable collapse, paving the way to an Iranian nuclear weapon and shattered U.S. credibility around the world. The President's circular logic claims that the deal does not restrict Iran's path to a nuclear weapon for long enough, but U.S. withdrawal would allow Iran to immediately restart its nuclear program. Trump's assertion that the deal does not constrain Iran's non-nuclear malign behavior is a complete non-sequitur. Ripping up the deal would not constrain those activities, and could embolden Tehran to enhance them.

By all accounts, Iran is in compliance with the JCPOA, and the deal is accomplishing a critical national security priority – preventing Iran from obtaining a nuclear weapon. Pursuant to the terms of the agreement, Iran has poured concrete into its plutonium reactor, reduced its centrifuges from 19,000 to 6,104, reduced its stockpile of enriched uranium to no more than 300 kilograms enriched no higher than 3.67 percent, and submitted to continuous monitoring and inspections at its key nuclear facilities. The International Atomic Energy Agency has released eleven verification and monitoring reports indicating that Iran has not violated the agreement, and the President has certified to Congress six times that Iran is in compliance.

Critics of the JCPOA charge that it is not an all-encompassing agreement addressing all of Iran's malign behavior, but abandoning the deal does nothing to counter these real threats. Iran's repeated testing of ballistic missiles runs contrary to the United Nations Security Council Resolution 2231. Iran's Islamic Revolutionary Guard Corps (IRGC) continues to bankroll and arm regional terrorist organizations, including Hezbollah and Hamas, that threaten our greatest ally in the Middle East, Israel. Iran further acts as a destabilizing force in the region by supporting the Houthis in Yemen and Shia militias in Iraq and Syria. And on the home front, the Iranian regime engages in significant human rights abuses to maintain its brutal stranglehold on the Iranian people.

Each of these behaviors constitutes a threat to the United States and therefore demands an appropriate response. That is precisely why we enacted the Countering America's Adversaries Through Sanctions Act (P.L. 115-44), which is the most robust sanctions regime ever passed by Congress. If President Trump shares my concern for Iran's other destabilizing behavior, then he should employ the authorities granted him under that law, which the administration has failed to implement. Trump has no overarching strategy to counter Iran's behavior and his administration's unilateral retreat has left a vacuum in Syria. There are serious concerns that the Syrian de-escalation zones, negotiated by the Trump Administration and Russia, have allowed Iran to operate freely on Israel's border.

Trump's October 2017 decision to decertify Iran's compliance with the agreement has reignited the previously contained threat of a nuclear Tehran. If the Administration reimposes nuclear sanctions on Iran, violating U.S. commitments under the deal, it will enable that which we all can agree is an unacceptable outcome – a nuclear-armed Iran. Withdrawing from the JCPOA allows Iran to immediately restart its nuclear program, and leaves the United States with only military options to combat Iranian nuclear proliferation. The last thing the world needs right now is an additional nuclear front. In order to prevent such a dire result, Congress must work in concert with the Administration to ensure that the nuclear agreement is fully implemented and strictly enforced.

To this end, I have reintroduced bipartisan legislation with my Republican colleague Rep. Francis Rooney to establish a Congressional-Executive Commission to verify Iran's compliance with its obligations under the deal. The Commission to Verify Iranian Nuclear Compliance Act (H.R. 3810) would ensure close and enduring Congressional oversight of the JCPOA as well as coordination between Congress and the Administration regarding implementation of the deal. Congress should act immediately to advance one of the rare proposals on Capitol Hill that has garnered support from both sides of the heated JCPOA debate.

Withdrawing from the deal would damage U.S. credibility in the eyes of our allies and adversaries and weaken our leverage to negotiate future agreements with Iran or other states. As the Administration prepares for a high-risk diplomatic summit with North Korea over its nuclear program, breaking America's commitments under another nuclear agreement signals that the United States cannot be trusted. The leaders of all parties to the Iran deal, including many members of Trump's own administration, maintain that Iran is in compliance. Chairman of the Joint Chiefs of Staff General Joseph Dunford reiterated that "Iran is not in material breach of the agreement, and I do believe the agreement to date has delayed the development of a nuclear capability by Iran." Secretary of Defense Jim Mattis added that the JCPOA included "pretty robust verification." This week, Senator Mac Thornberry, Chairman of the House Armed Services Committee, said that he "would counsel against" pulling out of the agreement.

If the President abandons U.S. commitments under the Iran nuclear deal, then he is responsible for the fallout. Without American participation, the deal will likely collapse. Our allies and adversaries alike will not trust American leadership to negotiate another agreement whether on Iran or North Korea or elsewhere. Our withdrawal would severely weaken U.S. leverage to avert a nuclear-armed Iran or to curb Iran's other abhorrent behavior. President Trump's manufactured crisis has serious and extended consequences that would harm U.S. national security for years to come.

**Question for the Record from Representative Dina Titus**
Confronting the Iranian Challenge
*For the Honorable Jane Harman*
May 8, 2018

## Question:

I share many of the concerns outlined in your testimony. Our European allies have tried to work with the Administration and make the case for why the U.S. should remain in the deal, but I do not feel confident he will listen to them after calling it one of the worst agreements in history during the campaign, failing to certify Iran's compliance in October, and suggesting ultimatums in January. As we know, this is not the only multilateral negotiation in which the Administration is currently involved. How does withdrawing from the JCPOA undermine our credibility on the global stage, and how can anyone trust the Administration on future negotiations, particularly with North Korea on denuclearization, if the Administration fails to uphold its end of multilateral agreements?

## Answer:

I think withdrawal was unnecessary and unwise. It angered our European allies and emboldened China, Russia and Iran. Iran's nuclear program was frozen for another 7 ½ years (out of 10), ample time to negotiate improvements to the deal and to impose tougher sanctions on Iran's malign behavior outside the deal. I also worry that this action will make it harder to negotiate a tougher deal with North Korea, the highest priority of this Administration.

www.ingramcontent.com/pod-product-compliance
Lightning Source LLC
Chambersburg PA
CBHW080033260726
48658CB00007B/2591